MICHAEL'S
GENUINE
FOOD

MICHAEL'S GENUINE FOOD

DOWN-TO-EARTH COOKING
FOR PEOPLE WHO LOVE TO EAT

MICHAEL SCHWARTZ
AND JOANN CIANCIULLI

WITHDRAWN

CLARKSON POTTER/PUBLISHERS
NEW YORK

Published in the United States by Clarkson Potter/Publishers, an imprint of
the Crown Publishing Group, a division of Random House, Inc., New York.
www.crownpublishing.com
www.clarksonpotter.com

CLARKSON POTTER is a trademark and POTTER with colophon is a
registered trademark of Random House, Inc.

Library of Congress Cataloging-in-Publication Data
Schwartz, Michael, 1964–
    Michael's genuine food / Michael Schwartz. — 1st ed.
        p.   cm.
    Includes index.
    1. Cookery, American.   2. Cookery, International.
    3. Michael's Genuine Food & Drink (Restaurant)   I. Title.
    TX715.S1457135 2010
    61.5973—dc22   2010008560

ISBN 978-0-307-59137-1

Printed in China

Design by Stephanie Huntwork
Jacket design by Stephanie Huntwork
Jacket photographs by Ben Fink

10 9 8 7 6 5 4 3 2 1

First Edition

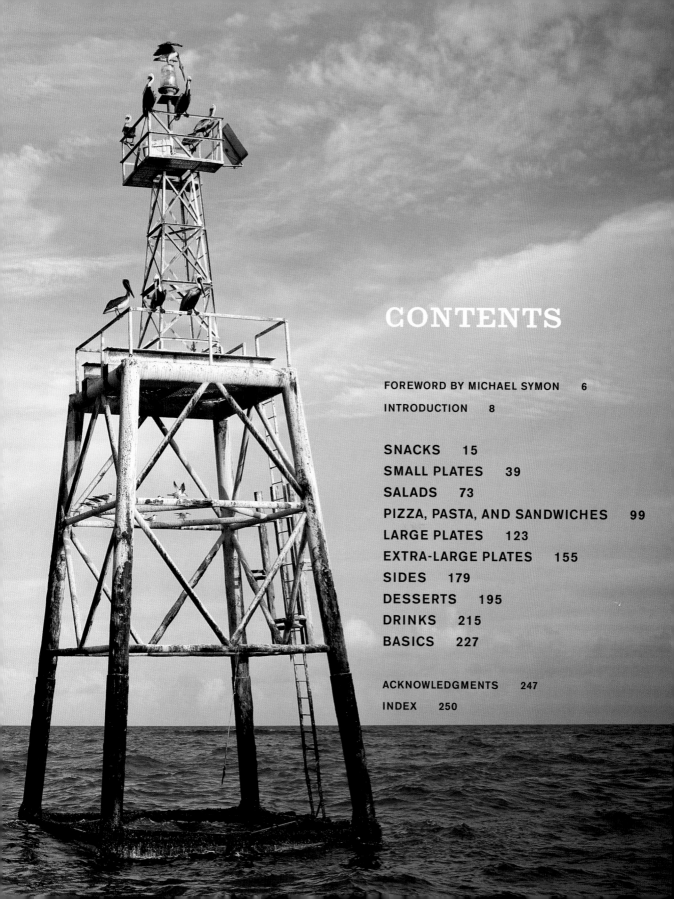

CONTENTS

FOREWORD

MICHAEL SCHWARTZ is one of my favorite chefs in the country—period. And as soon as I think about going to Michael's Genuine Food & Drink, I immediately start to smile since I know I am in for a great culinary adventure without pretension. From the minute I walk in the door, I feel the passion—it's oozing out of the restaurant from the giant stack of local seasonal vegetables on the counter to the warmth of the wood-burning oven—and know I am in for a treat.

To me, the greatest food can be recognized by what you feel when you eat it; when you can sense the personality and dedication of the chef in every dish—that's truly special. This is something that Michael brings to every plate, whether his playful spin on a BLT salad with maple-cured bacon that brings you back to your childhood, his soul-satisfying grilled leg of lamb that is so delicious it would make even my Greek mother swoon, or that magical baked double-yolk egg that shows you just how connected he is to local farmers.

The thing I love about Michael is that his cooking is whimsical without being silly. At its heart, Michael's food is simple, boldly flavored, and straightforward, which makes it not only fun to cook for a chef like myself but also very approachable and foolproof for the home cook as well. It is steeped in great technique and will teach you how to cook—just as if you've worked alongside Michael. As you make your way through this book you will immediately feel a connection to Michael, whether you have met him or not. That's a sign of a truly great cookbook.

Michael's credo towards food is one everyone should share: you are only as good as your ingredients. And as you read this book you will notice the care he puts into finding the very best. When Michael gushes over a perfectly juicy heirloom tomato, take that as a cue to head to your nearest farmers' market and buy food that is both seasonal and local. It will immediately make your cooking taste better and will help put you in touch with the seasons, which ultimately will make you a better cook.

There is not much in life better than a good party. When you open this book, you feel as if you are not only part of the fun—just like when dining at Michael's Genuine—but also that you can rock it out yourself at home. Here are the recipes and tips you need to get things going, from putting some snacks on the table in a hurry and making some killer cocktails to dropping down some extra large plates for everyone to enjoy. So come on in and join Michael's party where the food is fantastic, the drinks are cold, and the passion is genuine.

—**Michael Symon**

INTRODUCTION

PEOPLE OFTEN ASK ME if I cook at home and strangely they're always surprised when I say, "Yeah, of course, all the time." I find the question amusing because if I didn't love to cook I wouldn't be a chef. I do what I do because I live and breathe food . . . trust me there are far easier ways to make a living!

My wife, Tamara, our three children, and I live in a great house in a residential neighborhood in Miami Beach. While our kitchen is modest to say the least (no fancy range, mammoth fridge, or granite-topped center island), it's still very much the heart of our home. One of the ironies of being a chef is that I rarely get to actually cook at work. Cooking at home—and then sitting down with my family to eat—is very rewarding. When you break it down, cooking done with care is an act of love. As a chef, this is my time to play and prepare a wonderful triggerfish that my friends caught while spearfishing, or celebrate the bounty of each season delivered to our door by a local farm as part of our CSA (Community Supported Agriculture).

Sunday is our family time to cook and be together. For my kids, I make either something they really love, or something to open up their palates, but never anything too, too out there. This is food we all want to eat—like a BLT salad, grilled salmon, or maybe a whole roasted chicken. As a dad I totally dig seeing food and cooking through my children's eyes. My son, Harry, who is eight years old and my youngest, will experiment and try making anything, sometimes with reckless abandon. He is fearless and open to tasting everything. My middle one, Lulu, is a bit more of a finicky eater but loves to set the table and takes pride in her creative napkin folds. My teenage daughter, Ella, has been in the kitchen practically since she could walk so she has already developed her own palate and repertoire; she knows what she likes and what she doesn't.

I've been cooking since I was fifteen and I know what I like and what I don't. To define my food, I'd say it's an East Coast version of California cuisine. This book features grown-up, clearheaded dishes that are approachable, sensible, and affordable, yet still ones I love to make and eat—food that is elegant without being fussy.

I'm a believer in letting the ingredient and season dictate the dish. I've gotten tremendous support from the Miami community, which was ready to embrace the local eating movement, and that's what I'm all about. Farm-to-table is fairly new to South Florida and only recently have people discovered the great quality produce from surrounding local farms. I believe organic-regional-seasonal-sustainable is not just about doing the right thing; it's about doing it beautifully. Local food is fresher and tastes better than food that has been trucked or flown in from faraway places.

Buying food locally can also help create greater variety. Farmers who run CSAs, sell at farmers' markets, and provide ingredients to restaurants in the area have the demand and support from the community to raise different—and more—types of produce and livestock. Miami's natural bounty is unique to the region; take avocados, for example. There are over a dozen varieties grown here yet often Florida avocados tend to get a bad rap. People are familiar with the rich, creamy texture of California Hass avocados, which have large-scale distribution so you can get them all over the country. But Florida avocados, which are much bigger and fruitier, have a more complex flavor than that of the ubiquitous Hass; the Wilson Popenoe variety is one of my local favorites. I buy it because I love it and I buy it loyally so that I can help ensure it remains in production and on our plates.

Being a locavore is an important and necessary responsibility. I'm of the mind that everyone who respects what they eat becomes a member of Slow Food (www.slowfood.com). In the effort to spread the ideals of anti–fast food, the foundation brings together eating and responsibility, and makes them inseparable. If you care about where food comes from, how it tastes, and how our food choices affect the rest of the world, then you want to be in contact with others who care about those things too. At a certain point when you believe in a cause, you need to stop watching from the sidelines and get involved in the game, or else you're really missing the point.

One of South Florida's agricultural success stories is Paradise Farms, a beautiful five-acre certified organic farm located near Everglades National Park in Homestead, about one hour outside of Miami. Owned by a woman of the

earth, my friend Gabriele Marewski, this edible Eden grows the finest quality heirloom tomatoes, edible flowers, delicate greens and herbs, and a variety of tropical fruits including mangoes, avocados, and bananas. The 100 percent vegetarian bounty is harvested by hand; Gabriele doesn't even own a tractor. This biodynamic farm supplies some of Miami's best restaurants, including Michael's Genuine.

Shortly after Hurricane Katrina, Gabriele and I formed a charity-driven dinner series called Dinner in Paradise to raise money for worthy causes and create awareness of local farms, cuisine, and chefs. These are truly farm-to-table dinners, where notable chefs cook multi-course dinners outdoors on the farm itself, and guests dine right next to where the food was grown. The inspiration is to get people out of a restaurant environment and actually see how a farm operates and where the food comes from. We want to come full circle and close the loop—from the farmer, to the chef, to the diner. It doesn't get any fresher than that.

My unique involvement with Paradise Farms has inspired me to take "farm fresh" literally one step further and create Michael's Genuine urban farm. The design district in Miami is definitely not an agrarian landscape, yet I've borrowed a vacant lot across the street from the restaurant and turned it into a community farm. The goal was to take infertile ground and have it sprout into fertile land and use the organic produce to help supply the restaurant. The small but incredibly varied garden has beds of purple Cherokee tomatoes, French breakfast radishes, and petite greens like arugula, Asian tatsoi, and opal basil. The entire staff at Michael's Genuine takes care of the garden so everyone has a connection to the food being served. I hope to turn it into a weekly farmers' market open to the public in the near future.

The availability of farmers' markets is not limited to warm climates; they've propagated so that every local community has one. But if you can't take a trip to a market, be sure to shop wisely in your conventional grocery store. Today smart retailers are supplying the public's demand and bringing a greater variety of organics to supermarket shelves than ever before. Vote with your dollars! Sourcing quality ingredients may not always be convenient and can be expensive at times, but it costs more because it tastes better and is better for you. If you have to sacrifice that latte every morning to buy locally grown organic food, then it's an easy choice.

I kind of go nuts when people say to eat a tomato "only in July, the height of the season," because the growing season is completely backward down here in Miami; it starts in late November and extends through Easter. So our height of the season is the middle of winter, and that's when we find amazing local heirloom tomatoes, lettuces, radishes, and carrots, as well as some tropical fruits, such as passion fruit, guava, and jackfruit. (Year-round, we also get great local goat cheese, goose eggs, lots of grass-fed beef, heritage pork, and, of course, the best fish in the country.) In summer months, when it's too hot to grow some of those standard crops, we move on to other tropical fruits, including mango, lychee, papaya, banana, and avocado. And then we're lucky to be able to extend our reach up to northern Florida for summer staples like tomatoes, zucchini, and corn. Florida has the best of both worlds in one state. The key to seasonal eating is figuring out how to get the best near you whenever it happens to be in season.

One of my sayings is, "The secret to good food is . . . good food." I say spend more time shopping than cooking. No matter where you shop, always buy produce with the green tops attached, even if you think you are not going to eat them. The leaves are the telltale sign of how long something has been out of the ground or off the tree. Not surprisingly, I avoid buying any type of pre-packaged produce in bags, lettuce being the leader in the market. E. coli scares notwithstanding, the "quick and easy" greens get a chlorine bath leading to their distinct foul chemical odor—yum. Consider this: a bag of lettuce is three times more expensive than a head of organic lettuce. Is it really all that difficult to wash and dry lettuce in a salad spinner? Selecting excellent products is perhaps the most useful culinary skill of all and this vital wisdom can be implemented anywhere.

When I'm developing a dish, oftentimes it stems from the seasonal vegetable I picked up instead of the protein. If you go to the market and find beautiful Swiss chard, for example, build a dish around it and let it really sing. That's how the Swiss Chard and Caramelized Onion Panade (page 183) was born. If the chard isn't looking so hot, but the spinach is, go ahead and change it up. Have an open mind, and look for the freshest and best items available. Cooking is an evolutionary process and I'm constantly revising dishes, putting seasonal variations on recipes.

Food is not about impressing people—in fact it's just the opposite; it's about making them feel comfortable. The perfect meal is simpler than you expected and better than you remembered. Sometimes the best ingredient is the one left out. It is my sincere hope that this book captures genuine flavors and that you enjoy these recipes at home.

SNACKS

Whenever my wife, Tamara, and I have friends and family over, I always have at least one thing ready for them to nibble on when they walk in the door. As a rule, I'm not into precious individual hors d'oeuvres, because you end up spending so much time for so little result. You also won't find fancy-schmancy yet ultimately mundane frozen puff pastry, or prosciutto-wrapped asparagus at my house— or in these pages. A bit off the beaten path, imaginative noshes like Crispy Polenta Fries (page 21) and Kimchi Quesadilla (page 23) have guts and gusto. This chapter is loaded with my favorite snacks that can be mixed and matched, made ahead, and eaten with your hands.

CARAMELIZED ONION DIP
with thick-cut potato chips

MAKES ABOUT 2 CUPS ● A rich, creamy dip is a must-have for any good party. Make this onion dip ahead of time so the flavors can blend and mellow. If making the chips, for best results, you've got to cut the potatoes with a mandoline. If you don't want to fry your own potato chips, try one of the terrific brands in the market these days. This dip is also killer with crudités and pita chips, or even spread on a burger.

2 tablespoons extra-virgin olive oil

1 tablespoon unsalted butter

2 large onions (about 1½ pounds), thinly sliced

Kosher salt and freshly ground black pepper

4 ounces cream cheese, at room temperature

½ cup sour cream

½ cup Best Mayonnaise (page 246) or quality store-bought mayo

Chopped fresh chives

Thick-Cut Potato Chips (recipe follows)

Put a large skillet over medium heat and add the oil and butter. When the butter has melted, add the onions and season with ½ teaspoon salt and ¼ teaspoon pepper. Cook, stirring occasionally, until the onions are a deep golden brown and caramelized, roughly 20 minutes. Watch carefully—you don't want the onions to burn. Set aside and let cool.

In a large bowl, beat the cream cheese on low speed for 1 minute just until smooth and free of lumps. Mix in the sour cream and mayo. Fold in the onions with all their juices; season again with salt and pepper if needed. Cover and refrigerate for at least 2 hours or up to 2 days. Bring to room temperature before serving, garnished with chives, with a bowl of chips.

THICK-CUT POTATO CHIPS ● MAKES A BIG BOWL O' CHIPS (ABOUT 100)

2 large russet (baking) potatoes
  (about 1 pound), scrubbed
Canola oil, for frying

Kosher salt

Using a mandoline, slice the potatoes about the thickness of a nickel. You should get about 50 slices per potato. Put the slices in a large bowl and fill with cool water to cover. Swish the potatoes around to remove the excess starch; this will make the chips really crispy. Change the water 2 or 3 times until the water is no longer cloudy. Drain the potatoes well in a colander, then spread them out on a pan and pat dry with paper towels. This will prevent the oil from spattering from excess moisture.

Heat 3 inches of oil to 350°F in a countertop electric fryer or deep pot. If you don't have a deep-fry thermometer, a good way to test if the oil is hot enough is to stick the end of a wooden spoon or chopstick in it. If bubbles circle around the end, then you're good to go.

Put the potato slices in a fryer basket or spider strainer and carefully lower into the hot oil; do this in batches to avoid overcrowding and to keep the oil temperature constant. Give the potatoes a stir to keep them from sticking together. Fry the chips for 7 to 8 minutes, until they are golden brown and crispy. Remove the chips with the spider, allowing some of the excess oil to drain off, and set on a paper towel–lined platter. Season lightly with salt while the potato chips are still hot.

CRISPY POLENTA FRIES
with spicy ketchup

MAKES 2 DOZEN ● Golden and crisp on the outside with a moist, creamy interior, these polenta sticks, a modern twist on classic French fries, make a satisfying late-night snack or finger food. Making polenta is not as laborious as some would have you believe. It's not necessary to stand over the pot for an hour constantly stirring until your arm is falling off. The key to making perfectly cooked polenta is to stir often, running a wooden spoon along the bottom of the pot so the cornmeal doesn't stick and burn. This is an ideal make-ahead recipe; prepare the polenta in the morning and cut into sticks just before frying. For an outdoor barbecue, try putting the polenta on the grill; it adds a phenomenal smoky flavor. This salsa'ed-up ketchup is perfect to keep in the fridge for four to five days. The polenta fries and ketchup will happily join Michael's Genuine Burger (page 118).

1 quart whole milk

2 tablespoons unsalted butter

2 cups yellow cornmeal (not quick cooking), medium grind

1 cup grated grana padano or Parmesan cheese

Kosher salt and freshly ground black pepper

Canola oil, for frying

Spicy Ketchup (recipe follows)

Line a 9 × 13-inch baking dish with plastic wrap, letting the excess hang over the sides. Set aside.

Bring the milk, 1 cup water, and the butter to a simmer over medium heat in a large pot. Gradually whisk in the cornmeal in a slow steady stream. Reduce the heat to medium-low and switch to a wooden spoon. Cook, stirring often, until the polenta is very thick and pulls away from the sides of the pot, about 15 minutes. Remove from the heat. Stir in the cheese until incorporated; season with 1 teaspoon salt and ½ teaspoon pepper.

Pour the polenta into the prepared baking dish, spreading evenly with a rubber spatula; it should be about ½ inch thick. Refrigerate until completely cool and firm, at least 1 hour or, even better, overnight. It's important that the

(recipe continues)

polenta sets up completely and gets quite dense, so it's easy to cut into strips that won't fall apart in the hot oil when you fry them.

Heat 3 inches of oil to 350°F in a countertop electric fryer or deep pot. If you don't have a deep-fry thermometer, a good way to test if the oil is hot enough is to stick the end of a wooden spoon or chopstick in it. If bubbles circle around the end, then you're good to go.

Grab the ends of the plastic wrap and lift the polenta out of the baking dish and onto a cutting board. Flip the polenta over to remove the plastic. Cut the polenta into thirds lengthwise and then crosswise into sticks. You should wind up with 24 large Lincoln Log–like pieces, approximately ¾ inch wide by 4 inches long . . . yes, they're huge.

Put the polenta sticks in a fryer basket or spider strainer and carefully lower into the hot oil; do this in batches to avoid overcrowding and to keep the oil temperature constant. Fry the polenta sticks for 3 to 5 minutes, until they are golden brown and crispy. Transfer to a paper towel–lined platter to drain. Season lightly with salt while the fries are still hot. Stack the polenta fries like Lincoln Logs on a large platter. Serve with the spicy ketchup.

SPICY KETCHUP ● MAKES 2 CUPS

1 tablespoon vegetable oil
½ small onion, coarsely chopped
2 garlic cloves, coarsely chopped
1 jalapeño, seeded and chopped

Kosher salt and freshly ground black
 pepper
2 cups ketchup
1 tablespoon chopped fresh cilantro

Put a small skillet over medium heat. When the pan is hot, coat with the oil. Add the onion, garlic, jalapeño, ½ teaspoon salt, and ¼ teaspoon pepper. Stir until the onion softens and starts to get a little color, about 3 minutes.

Scrape the vegetable mixture into a food processor. Pulse until combined but not totally smooth; you want to keep the chunky texture. Transfer to a bowl and add the ketchup and cilantro. Mix together until well blended; season again with salt and pepper if necessary.

KIMCHI QUESADILLA

SERVES 2 TO 4 ● I know what you are thinking . . . kimchi quesadilla?! It may sound strange, but trust me: spicy kimchi and gooey cheese is a killer combo. You can assemble these quesadillas ahead of time and simply cook 'em up when you need them. Served with a simple salad, these also make a terrific light lunch.

Four 6-inch flour tortillas
¼ pound Monterey Jack cheese, shredded
   (1 cup)
1 cup Kimchi (page 233), chopped

Sliced scallion, white and green parts
Fresh cilantro leaves
1 lime, cut into wedges

Place a cast-iron skillet or nonstick griddle over medium-high heat.

On a work surface lay out 2 tortillas. Layer half of the cheese, the kimchi, and then the remaining cheese on each. Cover with the other 2 tortillas and press down with your hands.

Put the tortillas in the hot pan and cook until the bottoms are nicely toasted and the cheese begins to melt, about 2 minutes. Keep an eye on the heat; if the tortillas start to brown too quickly, reduce the heat to medium. Carefully flip the tortillas over with a spatula and gently press down—don't press too hard or the cheese will ooze out. Cook for another couple of minutes, until the undersides are golden and crisp.

Remove the quesadillas from the pan and cut into quarters. Shingle the wedges on a platter, garnish with the scallion and cilantro, and serve with the lime wedges.

FRESH HOMEMADE RICOTTA CROSTINI with apricot–thyme jam

SERVES 6 ● Luscious, juicy, and fragrant, apricots are one of the first signs of summer. The bright orange fruit is delicately sweet with a subtle tartness. Enjoy fresh apricots while you can—the season is short. Peaches make a fine substitute, however. This simple jam is made without messing with pectin and the list of ingredients couldn't be shorter. These crostini are truly the perfect bite: the toast is crunchy, the fresh ricotta creamy, and the apricots luscious and bright.

2 pounds fresh apricots (about 10), halved, pitted, and quartered
Juice of 1 lemon
1 tablespoon agave nectar

4 fresh lemon thyme sprigs
1 vanilla bean
½ cup Fresh Homemade Ricotta (page 236)
Crostini (page 27)

In a large pot, combine the apricots, lemon juice, agave, and thyme and place over medium heat. Split the vanilla bean down the middle lengthwise and scrape out the seeds with a paring knife; add them to the pot and toss in the pod too for added flavor. Bring to a simmer and cook, stirring often, until the apricots break down, about 20 minutes. To keep the jam nice and clear, skim any foam that rises to the top. Remove the vanilla pod and thyme sprigs. Cool the jam to room temperature. If desired, cover and refrigerate for up to 1 week.

To serve, spread a generous tablespoon of the ricotta on each crostini and top with a small dollop of apricot jam.

CHICKEN LIVER AND CARAMELIZED ONION CROSTINI

SERVES 6 ● A good recipe for chicken liver pâté is critical. This is not your grandmother's chopped liver; my version is supremely silky and light, with a hint of brandy. The chicken liver as well as the crostini toasts can easily be made a day ahead: refrigerate the liver, pressing plastic wrap directly on the surface, and store the crostini in an airtight container.

2 tablespoons unsalted butter

1 medium onion, coarsely chopped

Kosher salt and freshly ground black
  pepper

2 garlic cloves, minced

1 pound chicken livers, trimmed and
  rinsed

½ cup brandy or Cognac

1 tablespoon Dijon mustard

½ cup chicken stock

2 tablespoons heavy cream

Crostini (recipe follows)

Chopped fresh flat-leaf parsley

Place a large skillet over medium-high heat and add the butter. When the butter has melted, add the onion and sauté until caramelized, about 10 minutes; season with salt and pepper. Transfer a quarter of the caramelized onion to a plate and set aside for the garnish.

Add the garlic and chicken livers to the pan. Sauté for a couple of minutes until the livers begin to brown but are still slightly pink in the center; season with salt and pepper. Carefully, pour the brandy into the pan. If it flames up, shake the pan to put out the fire. Cook for a minute until the alcohol has evaporated. Mix in the mustard and stock, and continue to cook until the liquid is reduced by half, 3 to 5 minutes; it should still be pretty soupy. Don't cook the livers fully through as they tend to dry out and get a grainy texture. Stir in the heavy cream.

Transfer everything to a food processor and puree for a minute or two until completely smooth, scraping down the sides of the processor as needed; season again with a little salt and pepper. Set aside to cool.

To serve, spoon a generous tablespoon of the chicken liver on each crostini and top with the reserved onions. Arrange on a platter and sprinkle with parsley.

CROSTINI ● MAKES 24 SLICES

1 baguette, sliced ½ inch thick on a
 slight diagonal
Extra-virgin olive oil

Kosher salt and freshly ground black
 pepper

Preheat the oven to 350°F.

Brush the bread on both sides with olive oil and arrange side by side on a baking sheet; season lightly with salt and pepper. Bake until light brown and crisp, about 10 minutes. Flip the slices over or rotate the pan if some are cooking faster than others. Let cool completely. Alternatively, you can brown the bread on a hot grill or with a panini press, which will impart a light smoky flavor.

FALAFEL with tahini sauce

MAKES ABOUT 2 DOZEN FALAFELS ● Falafel, usually tucked into pita bread with lettuce, tomato, and tahini sauce, is one of the best-known Middle Eastern street foods. At home, falafels make a rustic hot hors d'oeuvre, with a bowl of creamy tahini sauce for dipping. These fry up just right: crunchy on the outside and fluffy in the middle. The baking powder gives the falafels a little lift so they don't sit in your stomach like belly bombs! All the fresh herbs make for a vibrant flavor and super green color. The chickpeas need to soak for a bit, so plan accordingly. The falafels are amazing with Quick Pickled Vegetables (page 235).

2 cups dried chickpeas, picked through and rinsed	1 teaspoon ground cumin
1 small red onion, coarsely chopped	1 teaspoon ground coriander
4 garlic cloves, smashed	1 teaspoon baking powder
½ cup coarsely chopped fresh flat-leaf parsley	1½ tablespoons kosher salt
½ cup coarsely chopped fresh cilantro	1½ teaspoons freshly ground black pepper
½ cup coarsely chopped fresh mint	Canola oil, for frying
	Tahini Sauce (recipe follows)

Put the chickpeas in a large bowl and add cool water to cover by 3 inches. Soak the beans in the refrigerator for at least 12 hours or up to 24; the chickpeas will swell to double their original size. Drain and rinse thoroughly.

Put the soaked chickpeas in a food processor and pulse until well ground (about the consistency of cornmeal). Add the onion, garlic, parsley, cilantro, mint, cumin, coriander, baking powder, salt, and pepper; process until the mixture is completely pureed, scraping down the sides of the bowl as needed. If you have a small processor, you will have to do this in batches, but be sure to combine the batches in a mixing bowl at the end so all the ingredients are evenly distributed. You can make the falafel mixture 3 or 4 days in advance; store it covered in the refrigerator.

Heat 3 inches of oil to 350°F in a countertop electric fryer or deep pot. If you don't have a deep-fry thermometer, a good way to test if the oil is hot

(recipe continues)

enough is to stick the end of a wooden spoon or chopstick in it. If bubbles circle around the end, then you're good to go.

Form the falafel mixture into golf-size balls with your hands. Be sure to press the mixture tightly; if the balls are too loose they'll fall apart. Carefully slip a few of the falafels at a time into the hot oil with a slotted spoon, gently nudging them so they don't stick to the bottom. Fry until the falafels are a crusty dark brown on all sides, turning as needed so there are no hot spots, about 5 minutes per batch. Remove the falafels with a slotted spoon and drain on a platter lined with paper towels.

To serve, arrange the falafels on a platter with a bowl of tahini sauce on the side for dipping.

TAHINI SAUCE ● MAKES 1 CUP

½ cup tahini (sesame seed paste)
1 tablespoon soy sauce
Juice of 1 lemon

2 garlic cloves, minced
Pinch of kosher salt

Combine the tahini, soy, lemon juice, garlic, salt, and ½ cup water in a blender. Process on high speed to make a smooth and creamy sauce. If the tahini sauce gets too thick as it sits, mix in a little bit of water or lemon juice to thin it out.

CLASSIC DEVILED EGGS

MAKES 24 PIECES ● Deviled eggs are a classic that doesn't need to be reinvented with all sorts of fancy ingredients. When it comes to making hard-boiled eggs, the biggest problem is easily overcooking them, which produces a nasty green ring around the yolk and a rubbery texture. The explanation for boiling eggs may seem like overkill, but trust me, you will have total success for the rest of your life.

1 dozen large eggs

¼ cup Best Mayonnaise (page 246) or quality store-bought mayo

1 tablespoon Dijon mustard

Juice of ½ lemon

2 dashes Habañero Hot Sauce (page 244) or store-bought hot sauce, or more to taste

1 teaspoon sweet smoked paprika

½ teaspoon kosher salt

¼ teaspoon freshly ground black pepper

¼ bunch fresh chives, minced

INGREDIENT NOTE

eggs

Buy local eggs! More than ever, farmers' markets are selling fresh eggs from heritage chickens. Well-treated chickens that spend a lot of time on pasture, getting exercise and fresh air, and eating green vegetables (which makes the yolk a deep orange color) produce tasty eggs year round. They often come in a rainbow of shell colors that denote the breed of chicken. The yolks of all should be bright orange and the white have body and sit up on itself. Pastured eggs may cost more than conventional eggs, but they deliver a lot more pleasure, are better for the environment, and leave you with a cleaner conscience (you would not want to eat most mass-market eggs if you saw how they are produced).

Put the eggs in a large wide pot, cover with 1 inch of cool water, and set over medium-high heat. Starting with cold water and gently bringing the eggs to a boil will help keep them from cracking. Once the water boils, turn off the heat, cover the pot, and let the eggs sit in the hot water for 15 minutes.

(recipe continues)

In the meantime, prepare an ice bath by filling a large bowl halfway with water and adding a tray of ice cubes. The key here is to cool the eggs quickly. Why? It's the best way to prevent discoloration around the yolk and it makes them easy to peel.

Using a strainer or slotted spoon, transfer the eggs to the ice bath. Allow them to sit in the water for 5 minutes so they are completely cool down to the center.

Give each egg a few gentle taps on the kitchen counter; you want to crack the shell without damaging the white underneath. Gently roll the egg around until the shell has small cracks all over it. Peel it off.

Using a paring knife, carefully trim off the ends of the eggs, so they will stand upright when serving. Halve the eggs crosswise (not lengthwise like you're used to seeing) and pop the yolks out and into a food processor. Add the mayonnaise, mustard, lemon juice, hot sauce, half of the paprika, the salt, and pepper. Puree until completely smooth.

Spoon the yolk filling into a pastry bag or a plastic bag with the corner snipped and pipe into the hollowed egg whites. Garnish the eggs with a sprinkle of the remaining paprika and the chives. Serve immediately or refrigerate, covered loosely, for up to 1 day.

GARLIC HERB BREAD TWISTS

MAKES 2 DOZEN ● Super addictive, these delicious soft breadsticks are laced with garlic, cheese, and herbs on the inside and out. They make a fun handheld snack that's a real crowd-pleaser. Serve them with Provençal Vinaigrette (page 240) or Lemon Aïoli (page 126) or just by themselves. Feel free to get creative and play with the ingredients, adding kick with chili powder or paprika, or for a Latin twist, try using cilantro, cumin, and cinnamon.

¼ cup extra-virgin olive oil, plus more for greasing the pans

3 garlic cloves, minced

1 cup freshly grated Parmigiano-Reggiano

¼ cup finely chopped fresh flat-leaf parsley

1 tablespoon finely chopped fresh thyme

1 tablespoon finely chopped fresh rosemary

½ teaspoon kosher salt

¼ teaspoon freshly ground black pepper

All-purpose flour, for dusting

Two 6-ounce balls Pizza Dough (page 232) or store-bought

Preheat the oven to 450°F. Lightly oil two baking sheets.

In a small bowl, stir together the oil and garlic. In another small bowl, combine the cheese, parsley, thyme, rosemary, salt, and pepper.

On a lightly floured surface, stretch or roll a ball of dough into a 6 × 8-inch rectangle. Brush the surface generously with some of the garlic oil and sprinkle with ¼ cup of the cheese-herb mixture. Fold the dough crosswise over itself, so the herb mixture is now tucked in the middle. Using a lightly floured rolling pin, roll out the dough to form a roughly 6 × 10-inch rectangle, about 1 inch thick. Repeat with the second ball of dough.

Using a pizza cutter or sharp knife, cut each rectangle of dough lengthwise into 6 strips, about 1 inch wide. Then cut the strips crosswise in half, so you end up with 24 pieces, each about 5 inches long. Grab each dough strip with both hands and twist both ends several times in opposite directions to coil into a twist. Place the twists on the prepared pan, 1 inch apart. Brush the twists with more garlic oil.

Bake the twists, rotating the pan halfway through cooking so they brown evenly, until golden, roughly 15 minutes.

Immediately after baking, roll the hot twists in the remaining cheese-herb mixture until well coated. Serve warm or at room temperature.

FRIED GNUDI with shaved parmesan and lemon crème fraîche

MAKES 3 DOZEN ● If you've never tasted gnudi before, you're missing out! Gnudi are small dumplings made with ricotta and Parmesan cheese mixed with flour and seasonings. The result is a delicate cheesy-pillowy morsel that literally melts in your mouth. They are absolutely incredible simply boiled and served with brown butter and sage, but I like to take things one step further by frying these little guys. Fried gnudi are an unusual, addictive party snack that feeds a crowd and is not at all difficult to make at home. I would describe the taste as a cross between gnocchi and a French fry. There's nothing better than that!

1 cup Fresh Homemade Ricotta (page 236) or store-bought whole-milk ricotta, strained
1 cup grated Parmesan, plus shaved for garnish
2 large eggs
1 large egg yolk
1¼ cups all-purpose flour
Kosher salt and freshly ground black pepper
Canola oil, for frying
Lemon Crème Fraîche (recipe follows)

In a food processor, combine the ricotta, grated Parmesan, eggs, egg yolk, ¼ cup of the flour, 1 teaspoon salt, and ½ teaspoon pepper. Process to form a smooth paste. This can be done a day or two in advance; store covered in the refrigerator.

Bring a large pot of salted water to a boil. Prepare an ice bath by filling a large bowl halfway with water and adding a tray of ice cubes.

Spread the remaining 1 cup flour on a plate. Using a small ice cream scoop, melon baller, or teaspoon, scoop the ricotta mixture into little balls. Don't worry if they are not perfectly round; as long as they're uniform in size, it's cool. Dip the scoop in water periodically to rinse. Lightly dredge the balls in the flour to coat, tapping off the excess. At this point, you can roll the gnudi in your hands to make them round.

Working in batches, slide the gnudi into the boiling water. Cook until the gnudi rise to the surface, about 2 minutes. Once they float, cook for another minute. With a slotted spoon or wire skimmer, transfer the gnudi to the ice bath. Repeat with the remaining dough. Remove from the ice water and pat dry with paper towels. The gnudi can be made a day or two in advance; store in a covered container in the fridge, drizzled with oil.

Place a large heavy skillet over medium heat and pour in an inch of oil. When the oil is hot, fry the gnudi in batches until golden on all sides, about 4 minutes. Don't move them around too much or they won't develop a nice golden crust.

Transfer to a paper towel–lined platter and season with salt and pepper. To serve, arrange the fried gnudi on a platter and top with shaved Parmesan. Serve the crème fraîche on the side for dipping.

LEMON CRÈME FRAÎCHE ● MAKES 1 CUP

1 cup crème fraîche	½ teaspoon kosher salt
Finely grated zest of 1 lemon	1 teaspoon truffle oil (optional)

Whisk together the crème fraîche, zest, and salt in small bowl. Cover and refrigerate until ready to use or up to 2 days. Right before serving, drizzle with truffle oil, if using.

SMALL PLATES

When I go out to eat, I usually do what most chefs do—order as many different dishes as I think I might possibly be able to put away. Getting to taste a lot of diverse stuff is my favorite way to eat. Sometimes I savor just a bite or two and sometimes I polish off my plate, but I never regret my choices.

Appetizers are your first chance to excite your guests and give them a hint of the meal to follow. Any one of these recipes will more than hold its own as a starter but if you're entertaining, serve a few together family-style. Small plates encourage sharing, allow for a reach across the table without hesitation, and provide the best topic of conversation—food. Some of these are light, some not so much, but all are damn delicious. Don't be surprised if you end up making the whole chapter.

ROASTED "DOUBLE YOLK" EGGS with tomato and asiago

SERVES 4 ● Are two yolks better than one? You bet! I have a real fondness for double-yolk eggs. In fact, I think every egg should have two yolks—I'm not an egg-white-omelet kind of guy to be sure. Luckily, there's a farmer in my area who farms nothing but fresh double-yolk eggs; it's pretty cool. Now, assuming you might not be able to get these, for ease, I've simply added extra yolks to the recipe. Crack the eggs into a ramekin along with some tomato sauce and cheese, and bake until the egg whites begin to solidify while the cheese turns into a cap of melty goodness. This makes a great start to a hearty meal and can elevate an ordinary steak-and-eggs dish to a special brunch. Make it ahead and pop in the oven when almost ready to serve.

4 large (about ½-inch) slices crusty
   sourdough bread
2 tablespoons extra-virgin olive oil
Kosher salt and freshly ground black
   pepper
1 tablespoon unsalted butter
¼ cup quality chunky tomato sauce

4 large eggs
4 large egg yolks
4 teaspoons heavy cream
2 teaspoons finely chopped fresh chives
¼ pound Asiago cheese, shredded (about
   1 cup)
1 small head frisée

Preheat the oven to 500°F.

Lay the bread slices side by side on a baking sheet, drizzle with the oil, and season generously with salt and pepper. Set aside.

Butter the bottom and sides of four 6-ounce ramekins. Divide the tomato sauce among the ramekins, then crack an egg and egg yolk into each. Add a teaspoon of cream to each and season with salt and pepper. Sprinkle with chives and add a layer of cheese to cover the top completely.

Put the ramekins on a baking sheet and set on the middle rack of the oven. Put the bread in the oven at the same time. Bake the bread until crisp, about 5 minutes. Bake the eggs until the cheese is melted and the egg whites jiggle a little when you nudge the ramekins, 8 to 10 minutes.

To serve, center the ramekins on small plates and lay a crostini on the side of each. Place a small mound of frisée on top of the bread.

ONION SOUP with garlic crouton, poached egg, and gruyère

SERVES 6 (MAKES 3 QUARTS) ● A few years ago my wife, Tamara, and I started raising chickens in our backyard in Miami. It's been a really fun experience and today we have eleven hens! With the coop comes lots of fresh eggs, so I'm always trying to find ways to use them creatively. This hearty onion soup is absolutely transcendent with a poached egg on top. When you cut into the egg, the runny yolk oozes into the soup, making it extra luxurious.

¼ cup duck fat or 4 tablespoons (½ stick) unsalted butter (see Note)

6 medium yellow onions (about 2 pounds), sliced ½ inch thick

4 garlic cloves, thinly sliced, plus 1 clove, minced

1 fresh thyme sprig

Kosher salt and freshly ground black pepper

1 quart low-sodium beef broth

2 tablespoons extra-virgin olive oil

6 baguette slices, about ½ inch thick

1 quart chicken stock

1 tablespoon sherry vinegar

6 large eggs

½ pound Gruyère cheese, shredded (2 cups)

2 tablespoons chopped fresh flat-leaf parsley

INGREDIENT NOTE

duck fat

I always keep a container of duck fat in my freezer and trust me, once you've tried pure rendered duck fat in your cooking you'll quickly make it a permanent staple in your kitchen. In fact, I gave a tub of it to one of my buddies for his birthday and he told me it was the best present he ever got! It's the gift that keeps on giving. Duck fat adds a layer of depth and richness to any recipe. Sub half of the butter in your favorite piecrust recipe with duck fat for added richness; fry potatoes, eggs, or even chicken in it. Duck fat truly elevates any dish and is especially terrific in this onion soup. It is available in gourmet markets and all over the Internet.

ut the duck fat in a large pot over medium-low heat. When the fat has melted, swirl the pan around to coat and add the onions, sliced garlic, thyme, 1 teaspoon salt, and ½ teaspoon pepper. Cook, stirring occasionally, until the onions are soft and tender and your kitchen smells amazing, 20 to 25 minutes. This is not the time to go check emails—keep an eye on the onions and don't allow them to get too brown.

Preheat the oven to 400°F.

Pour in the beef broth, bring to a simmer, and cook for another 10 to 15 minutes. Taste for seasoning and adjust if necessary. Remove from the heat and set aside.

Meanwhile, make the croutons. In a small bowl combine the oil and minced garlic. Brush the baguette slices with the garlic oil and arrange side by side on a baking sheet. Season with salt and pepper. Bake until golden, 5 to 8 minutes. Set aside.

Pour the chicken stock and vinegar into a wide pot and bring to a simmer over medium heat. When the liquid is just barely bubbling, carefully crack 1 of the eggs into a small cup or ladle and gently pour the egg into the stock. Repeat with the remaining eggs—you can easily poach 2 or 3 eggs at a time, spacing them apart in the pot. Poach the eggs for roughly 2 minutes, or until the whites are just cooked but the yolks are still soft. With a slotted spoon, transfer the eggs to a plate and dab the bottom of the eggs with paper towels to blot dry. Pour the poaching liquid into the onion soup. Bring to a boil.

To serve, preheat the broiler to high. Portion the soup into 6 ovenproof soup bowls or crocks. Place a crouton on top of each, then carefully set a poached egg on top. Sprinkle liberally with the Gruyère and place under the broiler until melted and browned, 5 minutes. Sprinkle with the parsley and a few twists of black pepper. Serve immediately.

TOMATO BREAD SOUP
with mini grilled fontina cheese sandwiches

SERVES 4 ● With only a handful of ingredients, this Tuscan peasant soup is deceptively simple, but tastes so rich and decadent, you'd swear there was cream in it. Heads up: blending the soup with olive oil is an important step to produce its velvety texture. The bread becomes suspended–almost like a custard–in the silky tomatoes; the basil adds a subtle perfume. Paired with nutty, gooey-smooth Fontina cheese sandwiches, this comfort food classic pushes all the right buttons.

¼ cup plus 2 tablespoons extra-virgin olive oil, plus more for drizzling

1 small onion, coarsely chopped

3 garlic cloves, coarsely chopped

Kosher salt and freshly ground black pepper

6 large beefsteak tomatoes (about 4 pounds), cored and cut into chunks

3 large fresh basil leaves

2 cups slightly stale crusty bread pieces (tear by hand)

Chopped fresh flat-leaf parsley

Mini Grilled Fontina Cheese Sandwiches (recipe follows)

INGREDIENT NOTE

beefsteak tomatoes

Virtually all of the nation's field-grown tomatoes come from Florida during the winter growing season. Big and beautiful, rich red beefsteaks are my tomatoes of choice. Balanced in both sugar and acid, their sunny fruit flavor and juicy sweetness shine with minor embellishment; there really is no substitute. I find Roma, or plum, tomatoes a bit too dry and mealy, and those little out-of-season tomatoes sold on the vine are full of water, have little to no flavor, plus are expensive to boot!

The best quality beefsteak tomatoes are not always available at major supermarkets. Seek them out at farmers' markets (or better yet, grow them in your garden or in patio containers, if that's an option). When buying, look for tomatoes with intense color that feel firm and heavy and smell like the plant itself. A slightly underripe tomato will ripen on the counter at room temperature. Do not refrigerate tomatoes; cold stops the ripening process, kills their flavor, and gives them an unpleasant mealy texture.

(recipe continues)

ut a soup pot over medium-high heat and pour in 2 tablespoons of the oil. When the oil is shimmering, add the onion and garlic. Cook and stir for a few minutes until the onion is soft; season with ½ teaspoon salt and ¼ teaspoon pepper. Add the tomatoes and their juices. Bring to a boil, then reduce the heat, and simmer until the tomatoes begin to break down into a chunky pulp, about 5 minutes.

Toss in the basil leaves and bread. Cook, stirring gently, until the bread gets very soft and absorbs the liquid, about 5 minutes. Push the bread pieces down with a wooden spoon if they float to the top. Reduce the heat to low, cover, and cook for 15 minutes.

Add the remaining ¼ cup olive oil and remove from the heat. Working in batches, ladle the soup into a blender. Alternatively, if you have an immersion blender, this is a great time to use it. Puree for a few seconds until completely smooth. Pour the soup into a tureen or other pot and season with salt and pepper as needed.

To serve, ladle the soup into bowls, drizzle with olive oil, and garnish with parsley. Serve the grilled cheese sandwiches on the side for dipping.

MINI GRILLED FONTINA CHEESE SANDWICHES ● MAKES 8 MINI GRILLED CHEESE SANDWICHES; SERVES 4

8 slices quality white bread
2 tablespoons unsalted butter, at room
   temperature

¼ pound sliced Fontina or Gouda
   cheese

ut the bread slices on a cutting board and butter one side of each slice. Place a large nonstick skillet or griddle over medium heat. When the pan is hot, add 4 slices of bread, buttered side down. Divide the Fontina among the slices. Top with the remaining 4 slices of bread, buttered side up. Cook, pressing occasionally with a flat spatula, until golden brown on the bottom, about 2 minutes. Turn the sandwiches over and toast the other side until the bread is golden and the cheese melts, roughly a minute. Transfer the sandwiches to a cutting board and cut each into 4 squares or triangles.

GROUPER CEVICHE with
mango, citrus, and cilantro

SERVES 4 ● Ceviche is a much-loved dish in Miami, with a million delicious variations. In a nutshell, it's seafood that is prepared by marinating in citrus juice, which makes the fish more opaque and firm, just as if it had been cooked with heat. I like to keep my recipe pretty straightforward and often use grouper, a favorite local fish. If you want to play around with other kinds of seafood, snapper, striped bass, scallops, and halibut are all the right texture. Whichever you choose, it's important to start with the freshest, cleanest fish possible. The bright, refreshing combo of orange, lemon, and lime with creamy avocado and sweet mango makes for a great balance of texture, flavor, and visual appeal. If I had to describe it, I'd say it tastes like sashimi salsa! A little of the kimchi base adds another level of pow. You can sub a good hot sauce but trust me; it's crazy good with the kimchi!

As with all cold preparations, all of the ingredients should be cold to start. Also take the time to chill your serving bowls to ensure the dish is enjoyed at the proper temperature. For a cocktail party, serve the ceviche in tablespoons or wonton spoons as single bites.

1 pound grouper fillet, skin removed, cut into ¼-inch slices

1 orange, seedless

1 lemon

1 lime

1 cup diced ripe avocado (see Note, page 52)

½ mango, peeled, pitted, and cut into medium dice

2 tablespoons finely diced red onion

2 tablespoons diced red bell pepper

1 tablespoon coarsely chopped fresh cilantro

1 teaspoon Momoya Kimchi Base (see page 233) or sriracha

½ teaspoon soy sauce

Kosher salt and freshly ground black pepper

Belgian endive, radicchio, or butter lettuce leaves

(recipe continues)

segmenting citrus

To segment orange, lemon, lime, or grapefruit, first trim the top and bottom of the fruit flat so it stands steady on a work surface; cut deep enough so you see the flesh of the fruit. Using a paring knife, cut off the skin and bitter white pith, following the natural shape of the fruit. Trim off any white areas that remain. Hold each piece of fruit over a bowl to catch the juices. Carefully cut along the membrane on both sides of each segment to free the pieces, and let them drop into the bowl. Then squeeze the remaining membranes over the segments in the bowl to extract the remaining juice. Remove any seeds.

Put the fish in a glass mixing bowl, cover with plastic wrap, and refrigerate while segmenting the orange, lemon, and lime (see Note).

Remove the fish from the fridge and pour the citrus juices into the bowl. Coarsely chop the citrus segments, particularly the orange, so they're about the same size. Put the citrus pieces in the bowl with the grouper. Add the avocado, mango, onion, bell pepper, cilantro, kimchi base, and soy. Season with salt and pepper and toss gently. Cover and refrigerate for no more than 15 minutes.

Line 4 small bowls with the lettuce of your choice, divide the ceviche among the bowls, and serve immediately.

KINGFISH ESCABECHE
with avocado

SERVES 4 ● Escabeche is a classic Spanish preparation in which you sear fish or meat, then marinate it in a vinegar sauce until it's sort of pickled. Unlike ceviche, which is raw fish "cooked" by citrus juice, escabeche is cooked first. The bracing and acidic vinegar cuts through oily fish such as kingfish (also called king mackerel), herring, or bonito just perfectly. This super simple dish makes a light, flavorful starter that wakes up the taste buds and hits the spot on a hot day.

½ cup all-purpose flour

Kosher salt and freshly ground black pepper

Four 3-ounce kingfish or mackerel fillets, 1 inch thick, skin removed

2 tablespoons canola oil

1 carrot, thinly sliced on a mandoline

½ small red onion, thinly sliced

½ red bell pepper, thinly sliced

½ cup sherry vinegar

1 tablespoon agave nectar

2 teaspoons mustard seeds, toasted (see Note)

1 bay leaf

1 fresh thyme sprig

2 cups 1-inch diced ripe avocado (see Note)

2 tablespoons extra-virgin olive oil

Fresh cilantro leaves

INGREDIENT NOTES

toasting spices

Put the spices in a dry skillet. Set over medium-low heat and toast, shaking the pan so the spices don't scorch, for just a minute to release the fragrant oils.

avocados

Living in Miami, I often use Florida avocados, which are really large, easily four times the size of Hass avocados, with a smooth green skin. Most people think they have no flavor, but I find that while they're not as creamy and rich as Hass, they possess subtle nuances of flavor—plus they're less expensive! Because avocados can vary greatly in size, I call for cup measurements in the recipes.

ombine the flour, 1 teaspoon salt, and ½ teaspoon pepper on a plate. Dredge the fish fillets in the seasoned flour, tapping off the excess. Put a large skillet over high heat and coat with the canola oil. When the oil is shimmering, lay the fish fillets in the pan and cook until well browned, 5 to 6 minutes. You want a good sear, so don't move the fish around, just let it do its thing. Turn the fillets over and sear until just about cooked through, 2 minutes. Transfer the fillets to an 8 × 8-inch baking dish. Scatter the carrot, onion, and bell pepper on top of the fish and set aside.

Put a small pot over medium heat and add the vinegar, ¼ cup water, the agave, mustard seeds, bay leaf, thyme, and 1 teaspoon salt. When the mixture reaches a boil, pour it over the fish and cover with plastic wrap. Marinate at room temperature for at least 1 hour or up to 8 hours in the refrigerator. If chilling, bring to room temperature before serving.

To serve, discard the thyme sprig and bay leaf. Divide the fish among 4 small plates and spoon the vegetables and the marinade on top. Scatter some chunks of avocado on top. Drizzle with olive oil and garnish with cilantro leaves.

GRILLED BACON-WRAPPED PEACHES with aged balsamic and piave vecchio cheese

SERVES 4 ● In my book, bacon-wrapped anything is good. Here crisp bacon and juicy peaches strike a perfect balance of salty and sweet. It's hard to beat a fresh-picked slurpy peach, but these little bites are a sexy way to dress up the luscious summer fruit, making for a sophisticated, beautiful small plate.

½ pound (twelve ⅛-inch slices) Maple-Cured Bacon (page 230) or store-bought bacon

2 large freestone peaches (see Note), halved, pitted, and cut into 6 wedges each

1 cup bitter greens, such as arugula

Fleur de sel or other coarse salt

¼ cup coarsely chopped pecans, toasted (see Note)

Piave Vecchio cheese (see Note)

Aged balsamic vinegar, Vincotto, or saba, for drizzling

Extra-virgin olive oil, for drizzling

INGREDIENT NOTES

freestone peaches

Look for freestone peaches, not clingstone. The pit pops right out of freestone peaches, while clingstone literally cling to the pit, making it hard to remove. If you can't find freestone, get the clingstone but just carefully cut around the pits with a paring knife.

toasting nuts

Preheat the oven to 350°F. Spread the nuts in a single layer on a rimmed baking sheet. Bake, checking the nuts periodically, until they are fragrant and lightly toasted, 8 to 15 minutes, depending on the type of nut. For example, pine nuts toast faster than pecans.

piave vecchio cheese

Similar to Parmigiano-Reggiano, Piave Vecchio is an aged cow's milk cheese from Italy but without the granularity. Its unique sweet and nutty flavor makes it a great addition to any cheese platter.

Preheat a gas or charcoal grill until very hot. Here is a great tip to keep food from sticking to your grill: Take a few paper towels and fold them several

(recipe continues)

times to make a thick square. Pour some olive oil in a bowl and dip the wad of paper towels into it. Carefully and quickly wipe the hot grates of the grill; this will create a nonstick grilling surface.

Lay the bacon on a cutting board. Set a peach wedge at one edge of each slice and roll up to enclose the peach. The bacon should wrap around the peach piece no more than one and a half times; otherwise it won't cook all the way through. Put the peaches on the grill, bacon seam side down. Grill the peaches, turning often, until the bacon is crisp, about 8 minutes.

To serve, put a small pile of greens on each plate and arrange the peaches on top. I like to sprinkle them with a tiny amount of fleur de sel. Scatter the pecans on the plates, and use a vegetable peeler to shave cheese over the peaches. Drizzle with balsamic and olive oil. The peaches are terrific hot or at room temperature.

JUMBO LUMP CRAB CAKES
with carrot butter sauce

SERVES 6 ● I know it's a bold statement, but this is the best damn crab cake you're ever gonna eat! Unlike most recipes, this one doesn't depend on bread crumbs or any other filler to hold the crab together. Sweet, succulent crab is mixed with not much more than butter and cream, which, when chilled, binds the crab cake together beautifully. When panfried, the outside gets crisp and brown while the butter melts inside, and what you bite into are warm lumps of luscious crab. When you want to pull out all the stops, this dish is impressive, elegant, and looks and tastes fantastic.

The crab cake mixture is best if made ahead so it has sufficient time to chill and harden. For an hors d'oeuvre, form the crab mixture into mini cakes. The super simple carrot butter sauce adds not only a bit more richness but also a subtle sweetness and vibrant color. Try it with grilled fish, too.

1 pound jumbo lump crabmeat, drained well, patted dry, and picked over for shells	⅓ cup heavy cream
	2 scallions, white and green parts, chopped
6 tablespoons (¾ stick) unsalted butter	1 cup all-purpose flour
1 small shallot, minced	1 large egg
1 teaspoon Old Bay seasoning	1 cup panko bread crumbs
Kosher salt and freshly ground black pepper	¼ cup vegetable oil
	Carrot Butter Sauce (recipe follows)
½ teaspoon dry mustard	Alfalfa sprouts (optional)
Pinch of cayenne pepper	

Put the crab in a mixing bowl and set aside. Combine the butter and shallot in a small pot over medium heat. Once the butter has melted, add the Old Bay, 1 teaspoon salt, ½ teaspoon pepper, the mustard, and cayenne. Stir to combine. Remove from the heat and whisk in the cream. Pour the butter mixture over the crab. Add the scallions. Fold the ingredients together gently but thoroughly, taking care not to mash the crabmeat. The mixture will look almost runny; don't worry, it will firm up in the fridge. Cover with plastic wrap and chill in the refrigerator for at least 1 hour; overnight is even better.

(recipe continues)

When ready to cook, use your hands to form the mixture into 6 crab cakes that are 1½ inches thick. They should be moist and just hold together. Put the crab cakes on a plate, cover with plastic wrap, and refrigerate while setting up your breading station. This allows the flavors to blend and the crab cakes to set.

To create a breading station, put the flour in a pie plate and season with salt and pepper. Crack the egg into a shallow bowl, add 1 tablespoon water, and beat with a fork until frothy. Put the bread crumbs in another shallow bowl.

Put a large skillet over medium heat, add a couple tablespoons of the oil, and swirl the pan around to coat the bottom. Working with 3 crab cakes at a time (keep the remaining cakes in the fridge), lightly dredge both sides of the cakes in the seasoned flour, dip into the beaten egg, and then coat completely with bread crumbs. Gently lay the cakes in the hot oil and brown for 3 to 4 minutes on each side (turning only once or they will break up). Drain on paper towels. Add the remaining 2 tablespoons oil, and repeat with the remaining 3 crab cakes.

To serve, pool ¼ cup of the carrot butter sauce on each of 6 plates, set a crab cake in the center, and, if you like, put a pile of sprouts on top.

CARROT BUTTER SAUCE ● MAKES 1½ CUPS

1 cup carrot juice	2 tablespoons heavy cream
1 small carrot, thinly sliced	8 tablespoons (1 stick) unsalted
1 shallot, coarsely chopped	butter, cut into chunks, at room
1 teaspoon kosher salt	temperature

Combine the carrot juice, carrot, shallot, and salt in a small pot over medium-low heat. Simmer until the carrot is completely soft and mushy, 10 minutes. The liquid will reduce almost, but not quite, by half.

Stir in the cream and simmer for 2 to 3 minutes to combine. It will look kind of a mess, a bit grainy and separated, but not to worry.

Remove from the heat. Whisk in the butter a few chunks at a time; all of a sudden, the sauce will come together. Pour the sauce into a blender and hold a kitchen towel over the top for safety. Buzz until completely smooth and a beautiful sunset color appears. Serve hot.

STOUT-BRAISED CLAMS
with potato, fennel, and bacon

SERVES 4 ● Clams steamed in beer is a favorite pub dish, and for good reason. The aroma of the hops in beer perfumes the shellfish and the malty flavor adds an extra roundness to the broth. Your kitchen will smell amazing! The sweetness of the clams, the licorice essence of fennel, the salty-smoky depth of bacon, and the slight bitterness of the stout make this a complex and flavor-packed dish.

¼ pound (four ¼-inch slices) Maple-Cured
    Bacon (page 230) or store-bought
    thick-cut bacon, cut into ½-inch pieces
¼ pound fingerling potatoes (about 4), cut
    into ½-inch chunks
½ small white onion, cut into ½-inch
    chunks
1 fennel bulb, top removed, fronds
    reserved, halved, cored, and cut into
    ½-inch chunks

3 garlic cloves, minced
½ teaspoon freshly ground black pepper
24 littleneck clams, well scrubbed
1 cup stout
1 cup chicken stock
2 tablespoons unsalted butter

Put a Dutch oven or large pot over medium heat. When the pot is hot, add the bacon and fry until it gets crispy and renders the fat, roughly 4 minutes. Using a slotted spoon, transfer the bacon to a paper towel–lined plate. Add the potatoes to the delicious fat left in the pot. Cook, stirring with a wooden spoon, until the potatoes get a little color and start to soften up, about 5 minutes. Add the onion, fennel, garlic, and pepper. Continue to cook until the vegetables are soft, about 5 minutes.

Raise the heat to high. Toss in the clams and pour in the stout and stock. Give everything a good stir and cover the pot. Steam until the clams open, 5 to 8 minutes, discarding any that do not open. Stir in the butter and sprinkle the reserved fennel fronds on top. Serve the braised clams from the pot, ladling portions at the table.

CHILE CHICKEN WINGS
with creamy cucumbers

SERVES 4 ● These may resemble traditional Buffalo wings in appearance, but a blend of soy sauce, tahini, ginger, garlic, and Asian chile sauce (available at Asian markets) makes these wings major-killer. This sauce is bangin' and can be used on grilled anything. Instead of typical celery and blue cheese, a cool side of cucumbers, Greek-style yogurt, and fresh mint finishes this dish.

½ cup sweet chile sauce, such as
   Mae Ploy
2 tablespoons tahini (sesame seed paste)
1 teaspoon rice vinegar
1 teaspoon soy sauce
1 teaspoon chopped garlic
1 teaspoon chopped fresh ginger

2 pounds chicken wings, preferably
   free-range
Canola oil, for deep-frying
Cilantro leaves
Sliced scallion
Creamy Cucumbers (recipe follows)

Combine the chile sauce, tahini, vinegar, soy, garlic, and ginger in a blender and process on high speed for 10 seconds. Set the chile sauce aside until ready to use or refrigerate for up to 1 week.

Cut off the chicken wing tips and discard. Split the wings in half at the joint to make wings and drumettes. Have your butcher do this if you want. Rinse the chicken wings and pat thoroughly dry.

Heat 3 inches of oil to 350°F in a countertop electric fryer or deep pot. If you don't have a deep-fry thermometer, a good way to test if the oil is hot enough is to stick the end of a wooden spoon or chopstick in it. If bubbles circle around the end, then you're good to go.

Carefully add the wings to the hot oil and fry in batches until they are crispy and float to the surface, 8 to 10 minutes. Transfer the wings to a large bowl. Add enough of the chile sauce to coat and toss well.

To serve, arrange the wings on a platter and garnish with cilantro and scallion. Serve immediately with the creamy cucumbers and the remaining chile sauce on the side for dipping.

BAKED CHILE CHICKEN WINGS ● If you want to go the healthier route, you can bake instead of fry the wings.

Preheat the oven to 500°F. Put the rinsed and dried wings in a mixing bowl. Coat with 2 tablespoons canola oil and season with salt and pepper, tossing to coat. Arrange the wings in a baking pan large enough to hold them in one layer. Bake, flipping them over halfway through cooking, until crispy on both sides, 20 to 25 minutes. Serve as directed.

CREAMY CUCUMBERS ● MAKES ABOUT 2 CUPS

1 English (hothouse) cucumber
1 tablespoon kosher salt
¼ cup Greek-style yogurt
2 tablespoons heavy cream
2 garlic cloves, minced

1 teaspoon chopped fresh mint
Juice of 1 lemon
¼ teaspoon freshly ground black
  pepper

Cut the cucumber in half lengthwise. Scoop out the seeds with a teaspoon. Slice the cucumber very thinly with a mandoline or a sharp knife. Put the cucumber in a medium stainless steel or glass bowl; add the salt and mix thoroughly to combine. Set aside for 10 to 15 minutes. Transfer the cucumbers to a colander and rinse thoroughly. Squeeze dry with your hands and then pat dry with paper towels.

Put the cucumbers back into the bowl and add the yogurt, cream, garlic, mint, and lemon juice. Toss to combine; season with the pepper. Refrigerate until ready to use or for up to 2 days.

ROASTED SWEET ONIONS
stuffed with ground lamb and apricots

SERVES 4 ● This Moroccan-inspired recipe is one of those dishes where less is more: a big, sweet onion stuffed with cinnamon- and cumin-scented ground lamb and plump apricots. While you may be tempted to put the whole spice cabinet in the lamb filling, the simple duo of cinnamon and cumin does the trick. The fruit plays off the rich gaminess of the lamb and the spices add a subtle background flavor to tie it all together. This stuffed onion is perfect for a weeknight dinner with a green salad and steamed basmati rice, or elegant enough to make as a starter for a dinner party. The best part is that you can do this all ahead of time and just pop the stuffed onions in the oven before dinner. Sweet!

4 medium Vidalia onions (about 3 pounds)

1½ cups chicken stock

½ cup dried apricots (about 16), cut into
   ¼-inch pieces

1 teaspoon finely grated lemon zest

5 tablespoons unsalted butter

½ pound ground lamb

1 teaspoon ground cinnamon

1 teaspoon ground cumin

1 teaspoon kosher salt

½ teaspoon freshly ground black pepper

3 or 4 shakes Habañero Hot Sauce
   (page 244) or store-bought hot sauce

2 tablespoons coarsely chopped fresh
   flat-leaf parsley

2 tablespoons coarsely chopped fresh
   mint

2 tablespoons fresh bread crumbs

Arugula leaves

Without peeling the onions, cut about 1 inch off the top of each and just enough off the bottoms so that the onions stand upright. Reserve the onion tops and discard the bottoms. Remove all but the outer two layers of each onion by scooping out the centers with a spoon or melon baller. Set the onion shells in a baking dish, along with the tops. Set aside. Finely chop the insides.

Preheat the oven to 400°F.

(recipe continues)

In a small pot, combine the stock, apricots, and zest over medium heat. Gently simmer until the apricots are plump and the liquid is reduced to ½ cup, roughly 10 minutes.

Melt 3 tablespoons of the butter in a skillet over medium-low heat. Stir in the chopped onions and cook until soft, about 12 minutes. Add the lamb, cinnamon, and cumin to the onions. Raise the heat to medium-high; season with the salt and pepper. Cook, continually stirring with a wooden spoon, until the lamb is crumbly, 7 to 8 minutes. Do not drain the rendered fat; you need it to keep the onions moist. Remove the pan from the heat. Stir in the apricot mixture with its liquid, hot sauce to taste, the parsley, and mint. Let cool slightly. The lamb filling can easily be prepared a day in advance, covered, and refrigerated.

Spoon the lamb mixture into the hollowed-out onions, pressing down with your hands to pack it in, and mound it over the onions. Sprinkle the bread crumbs on top and dot with the remaining 2 tablespoons butter. Cover the pan tightly with aluminum foil and bake for 30 minutes. Remove the foil and continue to bake for 10 minutes, until the bread crumbs are brown. Serve immediately with a few leaves of arugula on the side.

CRISPY SWEET AND SPICY PORK BELLY with kimchi and crushed peanuts

SERVES 6 ● Let me start off by saying that this not-to-be-missed dish . . . takes several hours to make. Even though the recipe involves a time commitment, someone who enjoys cooking will take pleasure in the process, and the end result is all the more satisfying. And I promise you, when you make this dish, it will blow everyone away! The succulent pieces of pork belly are melting on the inside and crispy on the outside. Spicy kimchi is the perfect counterpoint to the unctuous belly. Sweet, spicy, hot, cold, crispy, fatty, crunchy, and chewy—this dish has got it all.

3 pounds pork belly, skin removed, excess
    fat trimmed

¼ cup plus 2 tablespoons Momoya Kimchi
    Base (see page 233)

¼ cup honey

Canola oil, for frying

½ cup all-purpose flour

1½ cups Kimchi (page 233) or store-
    bought kimchi

3 tablespoons salted roasted peanuts,
    chopped

½ cup radish sprouts or microgreens

Score the top of the pork flesh about ¼ inch deep every ¼ inch in a cross-hatch pattern. Put the pork in a large baking dish and rub the meat all over with 2 tablespoons of kimchi base. Cover with plastic wrap and marinate in the refrigerator for at least 2 hours or, even better, overnight.

Preheat the oven to 325°F.

Remove the plastic wrap from the pork and replace with a piece of aluminum foil. Bake the belly for 2½ hours, or until the meat is super soft. Remove the pork from the oven and transfer to a platter or baking dish. Allow the meat to cool to room temperature, then cover and refrigerate for roughly 2 hours. Discard all of the pork fat left in the baking dish.

To prepare the glaze, in a small bowl combine the remaining ¼ cup kimchi base and the honey; set aside.

(recipe continues)

Heat 3 inches of oil to 350°F in a countertop electric fryer or deep pot. If you don't have a deep-fry thermometer to maintain the temperature, a good way to test if the oil is hot enough is to stick the end of a wooden spoon or chopstick in it. If bubbles circle around the end, then you're good to go.

Remove the pork from the fridge and cut into 6 equal pieces. Spread the flour on a plate and dredge all sides of the pork in the flour, tapping off the excess.

Using a slotted spoon, carefully slip 3 of the pork pieces at a time into the hot oil. Fry until the pork belly is crispy and brown on all sides, about 5 minutes. Transfer the pork to a platter lined with paper towels to drain. Repeat with the remaining pork belly pieces.

To serve, divide the kimchi among 6 small shallow bowls. Place a piece of the crisp pork belly in the center. Drizzle a little bit of the glaze on top and sprinkle with peanuts. Garnish with the sprouts.

CAPONATA with
pecorino romano

SERVES 4 TO 6 ● Similar to ratatouille, this Sicilian classic is a vibrant stew made with eggplant, roasted bell peppers, tomatoes, onions, raisins, and olives mixed together with lots of good olive oil. It's one of those dishes where the final product exceeds the sum of its parts. Fruity olive oil is essential to the success of this dish; it is the facilitator of all the ingredients. Caponata can be served warm or at room temperature, as an antipasto, a side dish, or a topping for Crostini (page 27) or pizza.

⅓ cup raisins

¾ cup plus 2 tablespoons fruity olive oil, or more if needed

½ fresh rosemary sprig

1 large firm Italian eggplant, peeled and cut into ½-inch pieces

Kosher salt and freshly ground black pepper

½ cup dry white wine, such as Sauvignon Blanc

One 14.5-ounce can fire-roasted diced tomatoes, drained

1 medium red onion, cut into large chunks

3 garlic cloves, minced

One 8-ounce jar roasted red bell peppers, rinsed and coarsely chopped

½ cup pitted green olives, such as Manzanilla, halved

½ cup fresh basil leaves, torn

Pecorino Romano cheese, shaved with a vegetable peeler

Preheat the oven to 300°F.

Put the raisins in a ramekin and pour in ½ cup of the oil to cover and 1 tablespoon water. Toss in the rosemary. Cover with aluminum foil and bake until the raisins are plump and the oil takes on some raisin color, 30 minutes. Remove from the oven and set aside to cool.

Put a large, deep skillet over medium-high heat and coat with ¼ cup of the oil. When the oil is shimmering, add the eggplant and cook, stirring often, until it gets soft and brown, 3 to 5 minutes; season with salt and pepper. Feel free to add a little more oil to the pan if the eggplant is looking too dry. Pour in the wine and cook until evaporated, about 30 seconds. Add the tomatoes, stirring to incorporate. Simmer for 5 minutes or until the mixture loses some of its moisture and the ingredients meld together.

Scrape the eggplant mixture into a bowl. Wipe out the pan with paper towels and return to medium-high heat. Drizzle with the remaining 2 tablespoons oil. Add the onion and sauté until soft, 3 to 5 minutes; season with salt and pepper. Add the garlic and sauté until fragrant, 1 minute. Scrape the onion mixture into the bowl with the eggplant. Add the red peppers, olives, and raisins with a few tablespoons of the raisin oil. Discard the rosemary. Toss in the basil and mix everything together. Serve topped with cheese shavings.

SALADS

There is something to be said about making a dynamite salad. When I was a kid, salad meant little more than a lame mix of iceberg lettuce, mealy tomato, and shredded carrot, topped with bottled dressing from the fridge. From being an uninspired course, thankfully the salad has evolved into one of the most varied and stimulating parts of a meal.

Salads are the perfect place to get your feet wet and start playing around with flavors. Use the recipes that follow as a solid guideline, but have fun and be flexible. Ultimately, let your neighborhood farmers' market be your inspiration to take advantage of the bounty of ingredients that are seasonal, fresh, and at their peak of flavor.

The salads in this book are creative affairs that can be served as a light prelude to a main course or as entrées themselves. Some don't even have lettuce! In my house, there is always a salad on the table. Eat your greens!

BUTTER LETTUCE SALAD
with orange, hazelnuts, avocado, and shallot-hazelnut vinaigrette

SERVES 6 ● Butter lettuce, as its name suggests, is so tender that it melts in the mouth like butter. Also called Boston and Bibb lettuce, butter lettuce should come as a fairly large, loose head with thick leaves and an even green color. I'm not a huge fan of hydroponic lettuce because you end up paying more for less lettuce, which makes no sense to me. Visit your local farmers' market or quality grocer and look for fresh, crisp leaves that are perky and not wilted. Butter lettuce is a terrific canvas to highlight the complementary flavors of acidic yet sweet orange, silky and dense avocado, and rich, crunchy hazelnuts. Shallot-hazelnut vinaigrette is my go-to multipurpose salad dressing; this recipe makes extra. Be sure to try it on other green salads or even grilled fish.

2 heads butter lettuce, wilted outer leaves discarded

2 navel oranges, segmented (see Note, page 50)

3 cups ½-inch diced ripe avocado (see Note, page 52)

About 3 tablespoons Shallot-Hazelnut Vinaigrette (recipe follows)

Kosher salt and freshly ground black pepper

¼ cup hazelnuts, toasted (see Note, page 54) and crushed

INGREDIENT NOTE

lettuce

If you are going to build a great salad, you have to start with great lettuce; there are more types of lettuce than cars! Salad mixes sold in the supermarket in bags might be convenient but they often harbor bacteria, despite being "triple washed" (often in chlorine–yuck). I encourage you to buy directly from a farmers' market or CSA (Community Supported Agriculture) or, even better, grow your own. Taste to see which varieties you like best—and mix and match crunchy and soft, bitter and sweet, red and green varieties for maximum impact.

(recipe continues)

Remove the core from the lettuce and break apart, tearing the leaves into smaller pieces by hand. Wash thoroughly and spin dry. Put the lettuce leaves in a large salad bowl. Add the orange segments and avocado, and spoon in enough dressing to lightly coat the lettuce. I beg you not to overdress and drown salads. Gently toss and season with salt and pepper. Divide among 6 chilled small salad bowls, evenly distributing the oranges and avocados. Top with hazelnuts and serve.

SHALLOT-HAZELNUT VINAIGRETTE •
MAKES ABOUT 1 CUP

1 small shallot, minced

2 tablespoons fresh orange juice

2 tablespoons champagne vinegar

2 tablespoons extra-virgin olive oil

¼ cup hazelnut oil

Kosher salt and freshly ground black pepper

In a mixing bowl combine the shallot, orange juice, vinegar, and olive and hazelnut oils; season with salt and pepper. Whisk thoroughly to combine. Keep any leftover vinaigrette covered in the refrigerator for up to 1 week.

GREEK FARRO SALAD

SERVES 4 TO 6 ● I'm crazy about farro's chewy-grainy goodness; this bright refreshing salad is the perfect complement to Grilled Leg of Lamb (page 163) and also makes a great little vegetarian lunch on its own.

1 cup farro	6 large basil leaves, torn into pieces
1 large tomato, cut into chunks	½ cup extra-virgin olive oil
1 English (hothouse) cucumber, halved, seeded, and cut into chunks	Juice of 2 lemons (⅓ cup)
½ red onion, diced	2 teaspoons kosher salt
1 yellow bell pepper, halved, cored, and cut into chunks	1 teaspoon freshly ground black pepper
½ cup pitted Kalamata olives	2-ounce block Greek feta

Bring a medium pot of salted water to a boil. Add the farro, reduce the heat to medium-low, and cover. Simmer until the farro is tender and the grains have split open, about 20 minutes. Drain and rinse with cool water. Put the farro in a mixing bowl.

Add the tomato, cucumber, onion, bell pepper, olives, and basil. Toss with the oil and lemon juice; season with the salt and pepper. Toss the salad to evenly distribute the ingredients. Put the salad on a nice oval platter, break up the feta with your hands, and scatter the chunks on top. The farro salad can be made a day or two in advance.

PERSIMMON AND POMEGRANATE SALAD
with crumbled ricotta and pomegranate vinaigrette

SERVES 4 AS A MAIN DISH OR 6 AS A STARTER ● A salad of unusual qualities, this vividly colorful combo celebrates the exotic autumn fruits of persimmon and pomegranate. The fusion of tastes is awesome: peppery watercress, sweet-spicy persimmon, tart pomegranate seeds, and salty cheese, all held together by a tangy vinaigrette. Leftover pomegranate vinaigrette will keep covered in the refrigerator for up to one week and goes great with grilled meats.

1 bunch watercress, stems trimmed (about 4 cups lightly packed)

2 medium heads frisée (about 8 cups lightly packed)

2 ripe Fuyu persimmons (see Note), peeled and thinly sliced

1 shallot, minced

¼ cup Pomegranate Vinaigrette (recipe follows)

¼ cup crumbled ricotta salata, homemade (page 237) or store-bought

¼ cup pomegranate seeds

INGREDIENT NOTE
persimmons

Persimmons are one of those fall fruits people often don't know what to do with. It's important to understand there are two kinds of persimmons: Fuyu (the kind you can eat right away), which is small and somewhat squat, and Hachiya (Japanese), which is shaped sort of like an acorn. Beware; if Hachiya persimmons are not completely ripe, they make your tongue do funny things! For this recipe I use Fuyu, which you can eat when firm, are crisp and sweet like an apple, and are really easy to work with. The shiny, pumpkin-colored fruit ranges from pale golden-orange to rich reddish-orange. Generally, the darker the color, the sweeter the taste.

In a mixing bowl, combine the watercress, frisée, persimmons, and shallot. Drizzle with the vinaigrette, tossing with your hands to dress the salad lightly and evenly. Divide the salad equally among chilled plates. Top with the ricotta and pomegranate seeds.

(recipe continues)

POMEGRANATE VINAIGRETTE ● MAKES ABOUT 1 CUP

2 cups pomegranate juice

¼ cup champagne vinegar

1 tablespoon balsamic vinegar

¼ cup extra-virgin olive oil

¼ cup canola oil

Kosher salt and freshly ground black pepper

Pour the pomegranate juice into a small pot and set over medium-low heat. Cook until the juice has reduced to ¼ cup and is thick and syrupy, roughly 20 minutes. Set aside to cool.

In a small mixing bowl or mason jar, combine the cooled pomegranate syrup, champagne and balsamic vinegars, and olive and canola oils; season lightly with salt and pepper. Whisk or shake to blend and dissolve the salt.

PANZANELLA SALAD
with heirloom tomatoes

SERVES 6 ● This rustic salad makes a substantial starter or a light lunch, and is especially nice when it's hot out. As with so much in Italian cuisine, the recipe is very simple; the key is the quality of the ingredients. The main attraction is featuring local heirloom tomatoes in peak season, which is summer to early fall in most places. Luckily, in Miami, we get locally grown tomatoes all winter long! It honestly doesn't matter how many varieties of tomato you use; the most important thing is that the tomatoes are ripe, juicy, and sweet.

½ cup extra-virgin olive oil

4 tablespoons (½ stick) unsalted butter

3 garlic cloves, thinly sliced

1 sourdough baguette or other good
    bread, cut into 1-inch cubes (4 cups)

Kosher salt and freshly ground black
    pepper

2 to 3 pounds assorted ripe heirloom
    tomatoes, such as Brandywine, Green
    Zebra, Sungold, and red beefsteak

2 tablespoons balsamic vinegar

½ cup fresh basil leaves, torn

Preheat the oven to 350°F.

Heat ¼ cup of the oil and the butter together in a small pot over medium heat. When the butter has melted, remove the pot from the heat and stir in the garlic. Put the bread cubes in a mixing bowl. Drizzle the garlic mixture over the bread while tossing to evenly coat. Season with salt and pepper. Transfer the bread cubes to a baking sheet and spread them out in a single layer. Bake, shaking the pan occasionally, until crisp and golden, roughly 15 minutes.

Using a paring knife, cut out the cores and carefully slice the tomatoes into somewhat large chunks and wedges. Put the tomatoes in a large bowl and add the vinegar, remaining ¼ cup oil, and the basil; season with salt and pepper. Add the warm bread cubes to the tomato mixture. Mix gently but thoroughly and adjust the seasoning if necessary. Transfer to individual shallow bowls or a large platter. Drizzle the vinaigrette remaining in the bowl on top and serve immediately while the bread is still slightly warm.

FLORIDA LOBSTER SALAD
with avocado, papaya, and jade dressing

SERVES 4 AS A MAIN DISH OR 6 AS A STARTER ● This mix of lobster, avocado, and papaya is a luxurious alternative to your everyday salad. It's sweet and creamy, perfect in the summer on a hot day. With the exception of cutting the avocado, all of the ingredients for the salad can be prepared ahead of time. Then, assembling the salad becomes a quickie. Leftover jade dressing will keep covered in the refrigerator for up to two days and is fantastic with grilled lamb chops.

Two ¾-pound spiny lobster tails, preferably fresh

Kosher salt and freshly ground black pepper

1 shallot, halved

1 teaspoon Old Bay seasoning

1 bay leaf

2 bunches watercress, stems trimmed

1 cup ½-inch diced ripe avocado (see Note, page 52)

1 cup papaya chunks

¼ cup Jade Dressing (recipe follows)

¼ cup pickled red onions (page 235), drained

¼ cup macadamia nuts, toasted (see Note, page 54) and coarsely chopped

To cook the lobster tails, fill a medium pot three-quarters of the way with water. Add 1 tablespoon salt, the shallot, Old Bay, and bay leaf; bring to a boil over medium-high heat. Carefully put the lobster tails into the boiling water and cook until the shells turn orange, 5 minutes. Using tongs, remove the tails from the pot and put them on a cutting board to cool.

Turn the lobster tails with the underside (the soft shell side) facing up. With kitchen scissors, cut lengthwise down the center of the shell and pull out the meat. Cut the lobster meat into ½-inch chunks. Transfer to a bowl, cover, and refrigerate.

In a mixing bowl, combine the watercress, avocado, and papaya. Drizzle with the dressing, tossing with your hands to dress the salad lightly and evenly. Season with salt and pepper. Divide the salad equally among 4 large chilled plates. Top with the pickled onions, lobster chunks, and nuts.

JADE DRESSING ● MAKES 1 CUP

1 large egg yolk (see Note)	¼ cup fresh cilantro leaves
¼ cup rice vinegar	½ shallot, coarsely chopped
½ cup canola oil	½ teaspoon kosher salt
¼ cup fresh mint leaves	¼ teaspoon freshly ground black
¼ cup fresh basil leaves	pepper

INGREDIENT NOTE

raw egg

The FDA suggests caution in consuming raw eggs due to the slight risk of salmonella or other foodborne illness. To reduce this risk, I recommend you use only fresh, clean, properly refrigerated, grade A or AA, preferably organic eggs with intact shells, and avoid contact between the yolks or whites and the shell.

Combine all the ingredients in a blender. Puree on high speed until thick and creamy and the color of jade, roughly 1 minute.

PEAR AND PARSLEY SALAD
with almonds and
creamy parsley dressing

SERVES 4 ● Parsley is the star of this simple green salad. It's not often that the herb, typically used as a garnish, shines as brightly as it does here, with a vibrant note that elevates the lettuce. The dressing is on the heavy side, so take care not to overdress the delicate lettuce. Leftover dressing will keep in the refrigerator for two days and is fantastic as a sandwich spread or a dip for chips.

2 heads butter lettuce, torn into pieces
2 ripe but firm red Anjou pears, halved,
    cored, and thinly sliced crosswise
½ cup fresh flat-leaf parsley leaves
¼ cup Creamy Parsley Dressing (recipe
    follows)

Kosher salt and freshly ground black
    pepper
¼ cup sliced almonds, toasted (see Note,
    page 54)

In a mixing bowl, combine the lettuce, pears, and parsley. Drizzle the salad with the dressing; season with salt and pepper. Gently toss to coat the leaves. Divide among chilled plates and top with the almonds.

CREAMY PARSLEY DRESSING ●
MAKES ABOUT ¾ CUP

½ cup Best Mayonnaise (page 246) or
    quality store-bought mayo
2 tablespoons Parsley Sauce
    (page 239)

Kosher salt and freshly ground black
    pepper

In a small bowl, mix the mayonnaise, parsley sauce, and 2 tablespoons water. Season the dressing to taste with salt and pepper.

BEET AND TOMATO SALAD
with green beans, blue cheese, and walnut vinaigrette

SERVES 4 AS A MAIN DISH OR 6 AS A STARTER ● I'll never understand why people don't like beets—they're wonderfully sweet and have a dense, meaty texture. When buying beets, I focus on what the leafy tops look like. The leaves should be fresh looking and dark green, not wilted. I shy away from baby beets, which I find to be unnecessarily pricey, as much as I stay away from huge rock-size ones. Heirloom tomatoes in a rainbow of colors add to this sunny summer salad—you won't even miss the lettuce! Like all the vinaigrettes and dressings in this book, the recipe will make a fair amount. Leftover walnut vinaigrette will keep, covered, in the refrigerator for up to five days. It's pretty thick and is ideal to spoon over grilled or steamed asparagus.

½ pound haricots verts (French green beans), ends trimmed

1 pound beets, tops trimmed, rinsed

2 pounds assorted ripe heirloom tomatoes, such as Brandywine, Green Zebra, Sungold, and red beefsteak, cut into chunks and wedges

½ cup Walnut Vinaigrette (recipe follows)

Kosher salt and freshly ground black pepper

¼ pound Danish blue cheese, crumbled (1 cup)

Bring a large pot of salted water to a boil over high heat. Prepare an ice bath by filling a large bowl halfway with water and adding a tray of ice cubes.

Blanch the green beans in the boiling water for only about 30 seconds; they become tender very quickly. Using a slotted spoon, remove the beans from the water and plunge into the ice bath to stop the cooking process and cool them down right away. This also sets their vibrant green color. Drain the beans in a colander and put in a mixing bowl.

Bring the water back up to a boil. Add the beets. Cover the pot, reduce the heat to low, and simmer for 20 to 25 minutes. To check for doneness, insert a paring knife into the centers; it should slide in without any resistance. Transfer

(recipe continues)

the beets to the ice bath as well. Once the beets are completely cool, rub the skins off with paper towels. If using red beets, it's wise to wear rubber gloves and put a piece of wax paper on your cutting board so you don't stain everything red!

Cut the beets in half or in quarters, depending on size. Add the beets to the green beans, along with the tomatoes. Dress with the vinaigrette, tossing with tongs to coat the salad evenly. Season with salt and pepper to taste. Divide the salad equally among chilled plates. Top with the blue cheese.

WALNUT VINAIGRETTE ● MAKES 1 CUP

½ cup walnuts, toasted (see Note, page 54) and finely chopped

2 shallots, minced

1 teaspoon Dijon mustard

3 tablespoons aged sherry vinegar

1 tablespoon balsamic vinegar

¼ cup extra-virgin olive oil

¼ cup walnut oil

Kosher salt and freshly ground black pepper

Put the walnuts, shallots, and mustard in a mixing bowl. Add the vinegars and whisk to combine. Slowly drizzle in the oils in a stream while whisking to emulsify the vinaigrette; season with salt and pepper.

BLT SALAD with maple-cured bacon

SERVES 4 ● I like taking foods I've grown up with and putting an adult spin on them. This knife-and-fork salad contains the elements of a BLT—bacon, lettuce, and tomato—but I replace the mayo with a big wedge of incredibly full-flavored Roaring Forties blue cheese. It's important for the bacon to be superthick, almost like a ham steak. If you don't make the bacon yourself, which is so beyond worth it, go to your local butcher and bring home slab bacon. There are only a handful of ingredients in this simple dish, but they are all important and shouldn't be skimped on.

¼ pound (four ¼-inch slices) Maple-Cured Bacon (page 230) or store-bought thick-cut bacon

½ shallot, minced

1 tablespoon sherry vinegar

3 tablespoons extra-virgin olive oil

Kosher salt and freshly ground black pepper

1 large head frisée, torn into bite-size pieces

2 pounds assorted ripe heirloom tomatoes, such as Brandywine, Green Zebra, Sungold, and red beefsteak, large ones sliced or cut into wedges

6 ounces blue cheese, such as Roaring Forties or Stilton, cut into 4 equal wedges

In a large skillet, cook the bacon over medium heat until crisp, about 3 minutes per side. Drain on paper towels. Cut the bacon slices in half crosswise.

In a large bowl, combine the shallot, vinegar, and olive oil; season with salt and pepper. Add the frisée and toss with the vinaigrette.

To serve, mound the frisée on 4 plates. Arrange the bacon, tomatoes, and blue cheese around the frisée.

GRILLED SKIRT STEAK with shaved fennel, orange, and green olive tapenade

SERVES 4 AS A MAIN DISH OR 6 AS A STARTER ● I love thinking of alternatives to your classic steak and potatoes. This main course salad is hearty without being heavy and contains all of the elements of a balanced meal—meat, starch, and vegetables. Grilled beef, crisp fennel, chewy fregola (see Note), and bright oranges are finished with a drizzle of briny green olive tapenade in this Mediterranean-inspired skirt steak salad.

Varying texture and temperature play a powerful role in the makeup of this dish, adding a whole other dimension. I'm a believer that opposites do attract; hot and cold—the grilled meaty steak and the cool crunchy salad—play off each other.

Tapenade is a rich olive spread popular in the Mediterranean. The salty earthiness of green olive tapenade is the perfect complement for pasta, spread for crostini, or topping for baked sweet potatoes. Visit your market's olive bar and purchase high-quality green olives; leave the little pimento-stuffed ones for martinis.

Four 8-ounce skirt steaks

2 tablespoons chili powder

Kosher salt and freshly ground black pepper

½ cup fregola (see Note)

½ large red onion, sliced ¼ inch thick

1 fennel bulb, top removed, halved, cored, and thinly sliced

8 radishes, ends trimmed, thinly sliced

½ pound arugula

Juice of ½ lemon

¼ cup extra-virgin olive oil

3 navel oranges, peeled and sliced into ¼-inch rounds

½ cup Green Olive Tapenade (recipe follows)

INGREDIENT NOTE

fregola

Fregola, sometimes called Italian couscous, is a terrific addition to your pantry. It's much more interesting than regular pasta and has a unique texture. The pasta dough is rubbed by hand to form little pellets, which are then toasted to give a distinctive nutty flavor. If hard pressed, you can use Israeli couscous, but there really is no substitute for fregola. It is worth getting your hands on. It also makes great risotto (page 116).

(recipe continues)

Lay the skirt steak flat on a baking sheet and season evenly on both sides with the chili powder, salt, and pepper. Set aside so the flavors can sink in a bit.

Bring a large pot of lightly salted water to a rapid boil over medium-high heat. Add the fregola and stir with a wooden spoon. Cook the pasta for 15 minutes until the pellets are al dente. Drain and cool.

Preheat an outdoor grill or a grill pan to medium-high heat. Rub the grill with oil to prevent sticking. Grill the onion slices for 2 minutes, turning often, until charred on both sides. Remove them from the grill and set aside.

Lay the steaks on the grill and cook, turning with tongs from time to time, to sear well on all sides; this takes about 8 minutes total for medium-rare. Transfer the steaks to a cutting board and let rest for 2 or 3 minutes to allow the juices to recirculate.

In the meantime, make the salad. In a large mixing bowl, combine the fregola, grilled onion, fennel, radishes, arugula, lemon juice, and olive oil. Toss to combine; season with salt and pepper.

To serve, divide the salad among 4 or 6 plates. Arrange 4 or 5 slices of orange on top of each plate. Cut each skirt steak into 3 equal pieces, then turn each piece sideways and cut into thin slices against the grain, ensuring tenderness. Shingle the sliced meat on top of the salad. Spoon some of the tapenade on top and serve immediately.

GREEN OLIVE TAPENADE ● MAKES ABOUT 1 CUP

2 cups pitted green olives, such as Picholine	2 garlic cloves, coarsely chopped
4 salted anchovy fillets, rinsed	1 teaspoon finely ground black pepper
	½ cup extra-virgin olive oil

Put all the ingredients in a food processor and pulse 3 or 4 times. Scrape down the sides of the processor and pulse 2 more times; the tapenade should be coarsely chopped. It will keep covered in the refrigerator for up to 2 weeks.

CRAB SALAD with ruby grapefruit, pickled radish, and pink peppercorn vinaigrette

SERVES 4 ● Grapefruit and crab are a classic combo; the addition of pickled radishes is both a colorful and surprising flavorful enhancement. Leftover vinaigrette will keep covered in the refrigerator for up to two days and goes great with all shellfish, particularly shrimp.

¼ small red onion, halved and thinly sliced on a mandoline (about ¼ cup)	Kosher salt and freshly ground black pepper
1 head green leaf lettuce, leaves torn	1 seedless ruby grapefruit, segmented (see Note, page 50)
¼ cup pickled radishes (page 235), drained	½ pound jumbo lump crabmeat, drained well, patted dry, and picked over for shells
¼ cup Pink Peppercorn Vinaigrette (recipe follows)	

Fill a small bowl with water and add 6 ice cubes. Add the onion slices and let soak for 5 minutes. This little trick removes the stinging bite of raw onion and makes the slices really crisp. Drain the onion and pat dry with paper towels.

In a mixing bowl, combine the onion, lettuce, and radishes. Drizzle with 3 tablespoons of the vinaigrette, tossing with your hands to dress the salad lightly and evenly. Season with salt and pepper. Divide the salad equally among 4 chilled plates. Arrange the grapefruit segments and crabmeat on top. Drizzle with the remaining tablespoon vinaigrette.

PINK PEPPERCORN VINAIGRETTE ●

MAKES ⅔ CUP

3 tablespoons pink peppercorns	¼ cup extra-virgin olive oil
¼ cup rice vinegar	¼ cup canola oil
1 teaspoon agave nectar or honey	½ teaspoon kosher salt

Blend all the ingredients in a blender on high speed until well combined.

CRISPY FISH SALAD with shaved red onion, mango, and soy-lime vinaigrette

SERVES 4 AS A MAIN DISH OR 6 AS A STARTER ● This gorgeous salad is the perfect balance of hot, sweet, salty, and sour that is the core of Thai cuisine. The cool mixture of mango, onion, and radish is topped with hot crunchy fried fish. This salad is downright addictive and will blow you away with its tastebud-awakening flavors and mix of textures. When cutting the fish, don't worry if the pieces are not perfectly uniform. Take note: this salad doesn't like to sit around, so serve it as soon as you can after you fry the fish. Leftover soy-lime vinaigrette will keep covered in the refrigerator for up to five days and is awesome tossed with chilled soba noodles or served as a dipping sauce for dumplings.

1 medium red onion, thinly sliced on a mandoline

1 mango, pitted, peeled, and chopped

5 radishes, thinly sliced on a mandoline

1 cup loosely packed fresh cilantro leaves

Canola oil, for frying

2 tablespoons all-purpose flour

2 tablespoons cornstarch

Kosher salt and freshly ground black pepper

1 pound firm white fish fillets, such as tile, snapper, or striped bass, skin on, cut into ¼-inch pieces

¼ cup Soy-Lime Vinaigrette (recipe follows)

Fill a small bowl halfway with water and add 6 ice cubes. Add the onion slices and let soak for 5 minutes. This little trick removes the stinging bite of raw onion and makes the slices really crisp. Drain the onion and pat dry with paper towels.

In a mixing bowl, combine the onion, mango, radishes, and cilantro. Stick the salad in the refrigerator while preparing the fish.

Heat 2 inches of oil to 350°F in a countertop electric fryer or deep pot. If you don't have a deep-fry thermometer, a good way to test if the oil is hot enough is to stick the end of a wooden spoon or chopstick in it. If bubbles circle around the end, then you're good to go.

Combine the flour and cornstarch on a plate and season with salt and pepper. Lightly dredge the fish in the mixture, tapping off the excess. Working in batches, put the fish in a fryer basket or spider strainer and carefully lower into the hot oil. Fry the fish for 2 to 3 minutes, until golden brown and crispy. Transfer to a paper towel–lined platter; season with salt and pepper while the fish is still hot.

Pour the vinaigrette over the mango salad, tossing to coat. Arrange the salad on a platter and top with the fish. Serve immediately.

SOY-LIME VINAIGRETTE ● MAKES 1 CUP

Juice of 2 limes (about ¼ cup)

3 tablespoons soy sauce

1 teaspoon hot sauce, such as sriracha

1 small shallot, finely chopped

One 1-inch piece fresh ginger, peeled and finely chopped

1 garlic clove, minced

2 teaspoons honey

¼ teaspoon freshly ground black pepper

¼ cup extra-virgin olive oil

Put the lime juice, soy sauce, hot sauce, shallot, ginger, garlic, honey, and pepper in a mixing bowl. Slowly drizzle in the oil in a stream while whisking to emulsify the vinaigrette.

PIZZA, PASTA, AND SANDWICHES

There is something innately familiar and homey about eating casual, unpretentious food. The downside is that comfort often comes with a lack of creativity and finesse, especially when cooking at home. It takes no effort to fall back on good ole standbys that everyone is used to. Boring! I consider the trio of pizza, pasta, and sandwiches its own dynamic food group with endless possibilities to have fun.

The approachable recipes that follow give rise to everyday fare, and are no more difficult or time-consuming than what you're currently cooking. Some dishes you may have already made, like fettuccine carbonara (page 114) or hamburgers (page 118), but the discovery is in the subtle details of tossing the pasta well to make it really creamy, and in adding a few tablespoons of ice water to freshly ground beef to keep burgers super moist. This fine-tuning makes all the difference, elevating food while putting a few modern twists on favorites you already know and love.

THREE-CHEESE PIZZA with grilled radicchio and fig

MAKES ONE 10-INCH PIZZA ● My kids, Ella, Lulu, and Harry, love making pizza at home and getting their hands in the dough. You don't need a special oven to make great pizza at home, although I recommend purchasing a pizza stone from your local kitchen store to ensure a crispy and crunchy crust. While you are at it, pick up a pizza paddle too. They often are sold as a set and run only around $30, so they're not a major investment. The pizza dough in Basics is extremely versatile and can be topped with basically anything you can come up with.

Here I wanted to come up with a vegetarian pizza that was so packed with interesting flavors, no one would miss the meat. Radicchio and arugula provide a slightly bitter balance to the melted and wondrous cheeses.

½ head radicchio

1 tablespoon extra-virgin olive oil, plus more for drizzling

Kosher salt and freshly ground black pepper

One 6-ounce ball Pizza Dough (page 232)

All-purpose flour, for dusting

¼ pound fresh mozzarella, preferably Fior di Latte (see Note), cut into small cubes

¼ pound Gorgonzola cheese, crumbled (1 cup)

5 dried Mission figs, stemmed and quartered

½ cup arugula leaves, stemmed

1 tablespoon grated Pecorino cheese

INGREDIENT NOTE

fior di latte

Mozzarella Fior di Latte literally means "milk of flower." It's a fresh cow's milk cheese made in a similar way to buffalo mozzarella. I prefer it because the flavor is subtle and delicate, even floral. You can find the creamy white mozzarella balls packed in water at Italian markets and fine grocery stores.

Preheat the oven to 500°F. Put a pizza stone or a baking sheet on the middle rack and preheat it along with the oven for at least 20 minutes.

Preheat an outdoor grill or a grill pan to medium-high heat (alternatively, you can preheat the broiler).

Discard any limp or loose outer leaves from the radicchio. Halve the radicchio through the stem end. Drizzle the pieces with 1 tablespoon oil and season with salt and pepper.

Rub the grill with oil to prevent sticking. Place the radicchio on the grill (or in a baking dish under the broiler). Grill, turning with tongs, until the radicchio is lightly charred on all sides, about 4 minutes. You want the radicchio to still have some color and crunch.

Transfer the radicchio to a cutting board, cut out the core, and cut the leaves crosswise into 1-inch pieces.

To prepare the pizza, dip the ball of dough into a little flour, shake off the excess, and set on a clean, lightly floured surface. Stretch the dough with your hands, turning the ball as you press down the center. Continue spreading the dough into a 10-inch circle with either your hands or a rolling pin. Don't worry if it is not perfect; it looks homemade and rustic. Leave the dough slightly thick so the topping does not seep through.

Dust a pizza paddle (if you don't have a paddle you can use a rimless cookie sheet as a substitute) with flour and slide it under the dough. Lightly brush the outer edge of the dough with oil to create a sheen on the surface of the crust. An important tip: take care not to get any oil on the pizza paddle (or pan), or else when you try to slide the dough off, it will stick.

Spread the mozzarella evenly on the pizza and scatter the Gorgonzola on top, leaving about a ¼-inch border. Distribute the radicchio evenly over the cheese; it will look like a lot but don't worry, it will wilt down and shrink. Arrange the figs on top and season with salt and pepper.

Slide the prepared pizza onto the hot baking stone and bake until the crust is nicely browned, roughly 10 minutes. Transfer to a cutting board. Shower with arugula, sprinkle with the Pecorino, and drizzle with a little oil. Cut into slices with a pizza cutter. Serve immediately.

SHIITAKE MUSHROOM AND
CARAMELIZED ONION PIZZA

SHRIMP AND CHORIZO PIZZA

THREE-CHEESE PIZZA

SHRIMP AND CHORIZO PIZZA
with manchego cheese,
toasted garlic, and escarole

MAKES ONE 10-INCH PIZZA ● There are endless possibilities when it comes to topping pizza. Here, sweet shrimp meet spicy chorizo sausage, slightly bitter escarole, and salty Manchego cheese. The combination is out of this world! If you haven't explored making your own pizza yet, let this be one to try with the family.

1 tablespoon extra-virgin olive oil, plus
    more for brushing

2 garlic cloves, minced

¼ head escarole (see Note), cut
    lengthwise through the core

Kosher salt and freshly ground black
    pepper

One 6-ounce ball Pizza Dough (page 232)

All-purpose flour, for dusting

½ pound Manchego cheese, shredded
    (2 cups)

¼ pound small shrimp, peeled, deveined,
    and halved lengthwise

One 2-inch piece hard Spanish chorizo,
    skin removed, very thinly sliced

INGREDIENT NOTE

escarole

A wonderfully versatile green, escarole remains one of those vegetables that people aren't sure how to prepare. You can eat escarole raw in a salad, and I love it that way, especially with Creamy Parsley Dressing (page 87), but it's at its best cooked. It's less bitter than its cousins radicchio and chicory, and sautéing it mellows out the flavor, making it sweet and vibrant. Escarole can be pretty sandy when you take it home from the market; luckily it is easy to clean. Cut the escarole crosswise into ½-inch-wide strips and put it in a large bowl of water. Swish the water around; the sand will fall to the bottom of the bowl. Lift the escarole out with your hands and put on a kitchen towel to dry. That's it!

Preheat the oven to 500°F. Put a pizza stone or a baking sheet on the middle rack and preheat it along with the oven for at least 20 minutes.

Put a large skillet over high heat and coat it with the oil. When the oil is hot, add the garlic and cook, stirring with a wooden spoon, for only 10 to 20 seconds, until it just begins to lightly brown. You have to keep moving the garlic around the pan so it doesn't burn; if it does, start over because nothing is worse than the flavor of burnt garlic. Quickly add the escarole and season with salt and pepper. Cook, turning the escarole over with the spoon, until it wilts, about 1 minute. Remove from the heat, turn out onto a large plate or baking sheet, and allow to cool. If the escarole looks too wet, transfer to a colander and drain in the sink.

To prepare the pizza, dip the ball of dough into a little flour, shake off the excess, and set on a clean, lightly floured surface. Stretch the dough with your hands, turning the ball as you press down the center. Continue spreading the dough into a 10-inch circle with either your hands or a rolling pin. Leave the dough slightly thick so the topping does not seep through.

Dust a pizza paddle with flour (if you don't have a paddle you can use a rimless cookie sheet as a substitute) and slide it under the dough. Lightly brush the outer edge of the dough with oil to create a sheen on the surface of the crust. An important tip: take care not to get any oil on the pizza paddle or pan, or else when you try to slide the dough off, it will stick.

Spread the cheese evenly on the pizza, leaving about a ¼-inch border. Distribute the shrimp and chorizo evenly over the cheese. Spread the escarole evenly over the top.

Slide the prepared pizza onto the hot baking stone and bake until the crust is nicely browned, roughly 10 minutes. Transfer to a cutting board and slice with a pizza cutter.

SHIITAKE MUSHROOM AND CARAMELIZED ONION PIZZA
with gruyère

MAKES ONE 10-INCH PIZZA ● What you put on your pizza is just as important as how much. It's about quality, not quantity. Don't go crazy and overload pizza with a jumble of toppings. Think about balance and a few well-chosen ingredients that work together. The Caponata (page 70) and the sugo (page 111) are delicious spread on pizza with a few cubes of mozzarella, for example.

Here earthy mushrooms matched with fragrant thyme and sweet caramelized onions pack this rustic pizza with major punch. Gruyère's robust and savory flavor profile knocks this no-sauce pizza off the charts. When it comes to pizza, this one delivers.

1 tablespoon extra-virgin olive oil

1 tablespoon unsalted butter

1 small yellow onion, halved and thinly sliced

Kosher salt and freshly ground black pepper

6 ounces shiitake mushrooms, stemmed and sliced (3 cups)

½ teaspoon chopped fresh thyme

One 6-ounce ball Pizza Dough (page 232)

All-purpose flour, for dusting

¼ pound Gruyère cheese, shredded (about 1 cup)

Chopped fresh flat-leaf parsley

White truffle oil, for drizzling (optional)

Preheat the oven to 500°F. Put a pizza stone or a baking sheet on the middle rack and preheat it along with the oven for at least 20 minutes.

Put a large skillet over medium heat and add the oil and butter. When the butter has melted, add the onion and season with salt and pepper. Cook, stirring occasionally, until the onion is a deep golden brown and begins to caramelize, roughly 10 minutes. At that point, add the mushrooms and thyme; season again with salt and pepper. Sauté until the mushrooms soften and begin to brown slightly, 3 to 5 minutes. Remove from the heat and let cool.

To prepare the pizza, dip the ball of dough into a little flour, shake off the excess, and set on a clean, lightly floured surface. Stretch the dough with your hands, turning the ball as you press down the center. Continue spreading the dough into a 10-inch circle with either your hands or a rolling pin. Leave the dough slightly thick so the topping does not seep through.

Dust a pizza paddle (if you don't have a paddle you can use a rimless cookie sheet as a substitute) with flour and slide it under the dough; it's easiest to top the pizza with the dough already on the paddle. Lightly brush the outer edge of the dough with oil to create a sheen on the surface of the crust. An important tip: take care not to get any oil on the pizza paddle or pan, or else when you try to slide the dough off, it will stick.

Spread the cheese evenly on the pizza, leaving about a ¼-inch border. Distribute the caramelized onion and mushrooms evenly over the cheese.

Slide the prepared pizza onto the hot baking stone and bake until the crust is nicely browned, roughly 10 minutes. Transfer to a cutting board. Shower with chopped parsley and drizzle with a little truffle oil, if desired. Cut into slices with a pizza cutter.

PAPPARDELLE with beef sugo and ricotta

SERVES 4 ● Slow-Roasted Boneless Short Ribs give new life to the idea of leftovers. Here, they're transformed into the perfect Sunday supper of ribbon pasta with succulent meat sauce. Once you prepare the short ribs, this dish takes relatively little time to make, yet your guests will be seduced by this sugo. The sauce will make more than you need, which you'll thank me for later. Store the remaining sugo in a covered container in the fridge or freezer. There is nothing worse than gloppy, oversauced pasta. Proportion is important; the pasta should be lightly coated in sauce, not drowning.

1 ounce dried porcini mushrooms, wiped of grit

¼ cup extra-virgin olive oil

1 large white onion, finely chopped

8 garlic cloves, minced

1 teaspoon chopped fresh thyme

½ teaspoon chopped fresh rosemary

Kosher salt and freshly ground black pepper

One 15-ounce can fire-roasted tomatoes

3 cups shredded, Slow-Roasted Boneless Short Ribs (page 148)

1 cup dry red wine, such as Cabernet Sauvignon

1 quart low-sodium beef broth

1 pound dried pappardelle

½ head escarole (see Note, page 106), cut lengthwise through the core

2 tablespoons unsalted butter

¼ cup freshly grated Parmesan cheese, such as Parmigiano-Reggiano, plus more for serving

¼ cup Fresh Homemade Ricotta (page 236) or store-bought ricotta

Chopped fresh flat-leaf parsley

To reconstitute the porcini, put the mushrooms in a bowl and pour hot water over them to cover, about 2 cups. Soak until the mushrooms soften, 30 minutes. Carefully lift the mushrooms out of the liquid with a fork, so as not to disturb the sediment settling at the bottom. Coarsely chop the mushrooms; you should have about ¾ cup. Strain the porcini soaking water into a measuring cup through a coffee filter or a double layer of paper towels; you should have 1½ cups.

Put a large skillet over medium heat and coat with 2 tablespoons of the oil.

(recipe continues)

When the oil is shimmering, add the onion. Cook, stirring, until the onion begins to soften, about 3 minutes. Toss in half of the garlic, all of the thyme and rosemary, and season with salt and pepper. Add the chopped porcini, the tomatoes, and the short ribs. Stir everything together and cook for about 5 minutes. Pour in the wine and continue to cook until the liquid has evaporated, roughly 10 minutes. Pour in the broth and reserved porcini water. Reduce the heat to medium-low and simmer for 1 hour, stirring occasionally. You should have about 6 cups of sauce.

Bring a large pot of salted water to a boil over high heat. Add the pappardelle, give it a good stir, and cook until tender but still firm to the bite (al dente), 8 to 10 minutes.

While the pasta is cooking, prepare the escarole. Put a skillet over medium heat and coat with the remaining 2 tablespoons oil. When the oil is shimmering, add the remaining garlic and stir until golden, only about 30 seconds. Add the escarole, stirring to coat with oil, and raise the heat to high. Cook, uncovered, stirring occasionally, until the escarole is wilted and most of its liquid has evaporated, 5 minutes. Season with salt and pepper. Add half of the sugo to the escarole and stir to combine. (Let the remaining sauce cool, then cover and refrigerate for up to 3 days or freeze for up to 1 month.)

To serve, drain the pasta and put it back in the pot. Add the escarole and sauce, along with the butter and Parmesan, tossing to coat the pasta evenly. Divide among 4 plates. Top each with a spoonful of ricotta and shower with chopped parsley. Pass more grated cheese at the table.

PENNE with pesto, white beans, and tomato salad

SERVES 4 ● This light summery riff on an Italian classic, pasta e fagioli, is as basic as it is tasty. I love the temperature contrast of hot pasta and beans with cool tomato salad, though you can also serve this peasant dish cold as a pasta salad.

2½ cups packed fresh basil leaves

1 cup fresh flat-leaf parsley leaves

½ cup grated Parmesan or Pecorino cheese, plus more for serving

¼ cup pine nuts, toasted (see Note, page 54)

4 garlic cloves, coarsely chopped

Kosher salt and freshly ground black pepper

½ cup plus 2 tablespoons extra-virgin olive oil

½ pound dried penne rigate

1 pint teardrop or cherry tomatoes, preferably a mix of red and yellow, halved lengthwise

½ shallot, thinly sliced

1 tablespoon red wine vinegar

One 15-ounce can cannellini beans, drained and rinsed

To prepare the pesto: In a food processor, combine 2 cups of the basil, the parsley, cheese, pine nuts, garlic, and ½ teaspoon salt. Pulse, pushing the basil down as needed, until a paste forms. With the motor running, add ½ cup of the oil and puree until smooth.

Bring a large pot of salted water to a boil, add the pasta, and cook for 8 to 10 minutes or until tender yet firm (al dente).

While the pasta is cooking, combine the tomatoes, shallot, vinegar, and remaining 2 tablespoons oil in a bowl. Stack the remaining basil leaves and roll them into a tight cigar-shaped bundle. Cut crosswise into thin ribbons. Add the shredded basil to the tomato salad, season with salt and pepper, and toss to combine.

When the pasta is almost done, add the cannellini beans to the water. Cook for only 30 seconds just to warm them up. Drain the pasta and beans in a colander, then transfer to a large mixing bowl. Add the pesto, tossing to coat everything evenly. Divide the pasta and beans among 4 plates and top with the tomato salad. Pass more grated cheese at the table.

FETTUCCINE CARBONARA
with crisp bacon and poached egg

SERVES 4 ● This dish was inspired by my friend and mentor Frank Crispo. To satisfy those deep creamy-pasta cravings, you're not gonna get more decadent than carbonara sauce. Pasta bathed in butter, oil, eggs, bacon, and cheese—it's a rich dish but enjoy it; you don't eat this every day.

1 pound dried fettuccine

1 tablespoon white vinegar

4 large eggs

¼ pound (six ⅛-inch slices) Maple-Cured Bacon (page 230) or store-bought bacon, cut into ½-inch pieces

1 tablespoon extra-virgin olive oil

1 tablespoon unsalted butter

4 garlic cloves, minced

1 shallot, minced

1 cup freshly grated Parmesan cheese, such as Parmigiano-Reggiano, plus more for serving

Kosher salt and freshly ground black pepper

Chopped fresh chives

Bring a large pot of salted water to a boil, add the pasta, and cook for 8 to 10 minutes or until tender yet firm (al dente).

Meanwhile, fill a wide pot with 2 inches of water and add the vinegar. Bring to a simmer over medium heat. Carefully crack 1 egg into a small cup and gently pour the egg into the water. Add a second egg and poach for roughly 2 minutes, or until the whites are just cooked but the yolks are still soft. With a slotted spoon, transfer the eggs to a plate, and blot the bottoms of the eggs dry with paper towels. Repeat with the remaining eggs.

Put a deep skillet over medium heat. When the pan is hot, add the bacon and fry until crispy and the fat is rendered, about 4 minutes. Add the oil, butter, garlic, and shallot, and sauté for 1 minute to soften.

Drain the pasta well, reserving ½ cup of the cooking water. Add the fettuccine to the pan with the bacon and toss well for 1 minute to coat it in the bacon goodness and create a thick, creamy sauce. Thin the sauce with a bit of the reserved pasta water, if needed. Sprinkle in the Parmesan and toss again. Season with salt and pepper.

Mound the fettuccine into 4 warm bowls and set a poached egg on top of each. Garnish with chopped chives. Pass more grated cheese at the table.

FREGOLA RISOTTO with shrimp, roasted corn, and melted leeks

SERVES 4 ● I'm crazy about the deep nuttiness of fregola (Italian couscous) and I'm always looking for new ways to show it off. When cooked in the style of a risotto, fregola gets really creamy and is a change from typical Arborio rice. Fresh corn turns this creamy risotto into summer goodness. The familiar flavors are boosted by the addition of shrimp and a topping of creamy melted leeks, which also makes a fabulous side dish on its own.

2 ears sweet corn, in the husk

2 quarts chicken stock

4 large leeks (about 1¾ pounds)

6 tablespoons (¾ stick) unsalted butter

2 fresh thyme sprigs

Kosher salt and freshly ground black
   pepper

¼ cup heavy cream

2 tablespoons extra-virgin olive oil

1 shallot, minced

2 garlic cloves, minced

1 pound fregola (see Note, page 93)

½ cup dry white wine, such as Sauvignon
   Blanc

1 pound large shrimp (about 20), peeled
   and deveined

2 tablespoons chopped fresh flat-leaf
   parsley, plus more for garnish

1 tablespoon chopped fresh tarragon

Preheat the oven to 400°F.

Put the corn in a small baking dish and add enough water to cover the bottom of the pan, about 2 cups. The moist heat cooks the corn perfectly. Bake the corn, turning the ears with tongs halfway through cooking, until the husks are brown and the corn feels tender when you press it, 40 minutes. When cool enough to handle, peel off the husks and remove the corn silks. Cut the kernels off the cob; you should have about 1½ cups.

Meanwhile, heat the stock until it simmers. Keep warm over low heat.

Cut off the dark green tops of the leeks and discard. Cut the leeks crosswise into ½-inch rounds. Put them in a large bowl of water. Swish the water around and separate the leek pieces, checking for dirt between the layers. The sand will fall to the bottom of the bowl. Lift the leeks out with your hands and put them on a kitchen towel to dry; you should have about 6 cups.

Put a large skillet over low heat and add 4 tablespoons of the butter. When the butter is foamy, add the leeks and thyme; season with salt and pepper. Cook, stirring occasionally, until the leeks are tender but not brown, 15 to 20 minutes. Remove the thyme sprigs. Pour in the cream and stir to incorporate. Cover and keep warm over very low heat.

Put a large, deep skillet over medium heat and drizzle with the oil, then add 1 tablespoon of the butter. When the butter is foamy, add the shallot and garlic. Cook, stirring, until the shallot is soft, about 3 minutes. Add the fregola and stir for a minute or two until the pasta is well coated; season with salt and pepper. Stir in the wine and simmer for 1 minute to evaporate the alcohol.

Pour in 1 cup of the warm stock. Stir with a wooden spoon until the pasta has absorbed all of the liquid. Keep stirring while adding the stock little by little, allowing the pasta to drink it in before you add more. This whole process should take about 20 minutes. You may not need all of the stock. Taste the risotto: it should be slightly firm but creamy. Add the corn, shrimp, parsley, and tarragon. Cook, stirring, until the shrimp are pink and cooked through, 3 to 5 minutes. Remove from the heat and stir in the remaining tablespoon of butter to make it rich.

To serve, divide the risotto among 4 shallow bowls, top with the leeks, and garnish with a shower of parsley.

MICHAEL'S GENUINE BURGER with house smoked bacon and vermont cheddar

SERVES 4 ● If you want a burger with superior flavor, you need to grind the meat yourself—it's as simple as that. The process is not only easier than most people think, but also makes the moistest and most flavorful burgers. You'll need to pick up a meat grinder attachment for your food processor at a kitchen store or have your local butcher grind the meat for you. Buy chuck with about 20 percent fat; if that's not available, kindly ask your nice butcher to add beef fat to regular lean chuck. Fat equals flavor, and there's no better place for it than in a burger!

Okay, you will also need to mix the meat in an electric mixer. It may sound odd, but an old butcher's trick is to add a couple tablespoons of ice water to the meat. As the burger cooks, the water steams, making the burgers juicier. With all of this love and attention to the meat, I don't think it's necessary to mix a bunch of stuff into it, like chives, chopped onion, or Worcestershire sauce. This meatier burger is as genuine as you can get!

1½ pounds beef chuck, freshly ground
Kosher salt and freshly ground black
   pepper
Canola oil
8 slices white Vermont Cheddar cheese
4 large brioche hamburger buns, split

Cooked Maple-Cured Bacon (page 230) or
   thick-cut store-bought bacon
Butter lettuce leaves, tomato slices, and
   red onion slices
Ketchup, Best Mayonnaise (page 246) or
   store-bought mayo, and Dijon mustard

Put the ground beef in the bowl of a standing electric mixer fitted with the paddle attachment. Add 2 tablespoons ice water and mix on low speed for 30 seconds. Gently hand shape the ground beef into 4 balls; 6 ounces each is about right. Don't pack the meat too tightly—you're not making snowballs here. Too much pressure will make a tough burger.

Place a large griddle on two burners over medium-high heat. Season both sides of the burgers generously with salt and pepper and drizzle the tops with a little oil. Put the burgers on the griddle, oil side down, and gently flatten once into big patties with the bottom of a spatula. Grill the burgers for 8 minutes per side for medium, 7 minutes if you like your meat rare. (If you like your burger well done, then I can't help you.) Flip only once and top with the cheese after flipping.

Serve the burgers on the buns with the toppings of your choice: bacon, lettuce, tomato and red onion slices, ketchup, mayonnaise, and mustard.

SHORT RIB AND FONTINA CHEESE PANINI with tomato-onion chutney

SERVES 4 ● The great bonus about making Slow-Roasted Boneless Short Ribs is that you'll have leftover meat to spin into this melt-in-your-mouth sandwich, panini-style. It hits the spot when you're in the mood for some serious comfort food. The Tomato-Onion Chutney is so freakin' good, you'll want to put it on everything. For starters, try it as a condiment with Whole Roasted Chicken (page 142).

1 tablespoon extra-virgin olive oil

Four ¼-inch slices red onion

4 ciabatta rolls, halved

½ pound Fontina cheese, shredded (about 2 cups)

3 cups shredded Slow-Roasted Boneless Short Ribs (page 148), warm

½ cup fresh arugula leaves, stemmed

1 cup Tomato-Onion Chutney (recipe follows)

Preheat a sandwich press according to the manufacturer's instructions. If you don't have an electric press, place a grill pan or heavy skillet over medium-high heat. Brush the pan with oil.

Lay the onion slices side by side in the hot pan. Grill on both sides until softened and slightly charred, 2 minutes.

When building the sandwiches, make sure to distribute the ingredients evenly across the bread so the sandwiches press flat. First sprinkle half of the cheese on the bottom half of the rolls, then divide the shredded meat on top. Add a slice of grilled onion to each, then add the remaining cheese. Put the other half of the roll on top.

Put the sandwiches in the preheated panini maker or grill pan. Close the press (or, if using a grill pan, place another heavy pan on top of the sandwich to press it down). Grill until the ciabatta is crisp on both sides and the cheese is melted, about 3 minutes. (If you cook the sandwich in a pan on the stove, after 3 minutes flip it over and then crisp the other side for 2 minutes.)

Transfer the sandwiches to a cutting board. Open them up, scatter a few fresh arugula leaves on top, and close back up. Cut the sandwiches diagonally in half with a sharp knife and serve with the chutney on the side for dipping.

TOMATO-ONION CHUTNEY ● MAKES 3 CUPS

4 ripe tomatoes (2 pounds), preferably
   red beefsteak, cored

¼ cup extra-virgin olive oil

1 pound cipollini onions (see Note),
   peeled and halved lengthwise or
   quartered, depending on size

2 whole cloves

1 teaspoon kosher salt

½ teaspoon freshly ground black
   pepper

¼ cup champagne vinegar

2 tablespoons agave nectar or honey

INGREDIENT NOTE

cipollini onions

Pronounced chip-oh-LEE-nee, cipollini are sweet, flattened, flying saucer–shaped onions from Italy. They have a distinctly crisp texture. The good news is they are becoming widely available in markets. If you can't find them, substitute pearl onions or shallots.

Bring a pot of water to a boil. Prepare an ice bath by filling a large bowl halfway with water and adding a tray of ice cubes.

Using a paring knife, cut a little cross mark on the bottom of the tomatoes. Immerse them in the boiling water for 15 to 30 seconds, until the skin starts to peel away. Using a slotted spoon, remove the tomatoes from the pot and transfer to the ice bath to cool quickly and stop the cooking process. Peel the tomatoes with your hands or a paring knife. Cut them in half and squeeze out the seeds. Coarsely chop the tomatoes and set aside. You should have roughly 3½ cups.

Put a large skillet over medium heat and coat with the oil. When the oil is shimmering, add the onions. Cook, stirring occasionally, until they soften slightly and get a little bit of color, about 5 minutes.

Add the tomatoes and cloves and season with salt and pepper. Cook, stirring occasionally, until the tomatoes start to break down and release their liquid, about 10 minutes. Add the vinegar and agave. Continue to cook, stirring often to prevent burning, until the liquid has evaporated and the chutney is thick, about 5 minutes. The chutney will keep covered in the refrigerator for up to 1 week.

LARGE PLATES

I don't like to overdo things. It's more like, how simple can I make this meal and still have everything fit together? I'm all about practicality, flavor, and time. I'm not interested in preparing a fussy dinner with a side of stress. That way, the world outside slows down just a bit, and I can connect with my family.

The main event of the meal, these entrées are the foundation for dinner; they're hearty, delicious, and straightforward to make. With the exception of the mind-blowingly flavorful Slow-Roasted Boneless Short Ribs (page 148), most of these dishes can be made in about an hour. So before you order in or get takeout, try these soulful and hugely satisfying recipes. I've always appreciated this quotation from the late gastronome Richard Olney: "The meaning of life lies in love and friendship, and those qualities are best expressed at the table." Please take a seat.

SEARED BLACK GROUPER
with pancetta roasted brussels sprouts and lemon aïoli

SERVES 4 ● One of the kings among Gulf fish is definitely black grouper; I'm always compelled to order it when I see it on a menu. The fish boasts a subtle sweet flavor and fine texture, its creamy white flesh just firm enough to hold together when you cut into it. Black grouper is caught locally off the coast of Florida and sadly is often overlooked around the rest of the country. If you can't locate some good grouper, striped bass or red snapper is a terrific substitute. The tangy lemon aïoli is a great all-purpose condiment to serve with poached shellfish or steamed vegetables. Here it also provides some relief from the richness of the dish, particularly the unctuous pancetta-coated Brussels sprouts.

1 cup Best Mayonnaise (page 246) or
    quality store-bought mayo
Juice and grated zest of 1 lemon, plus
    more zest for garnish
2 garlic cloves, minced
Kosher salt and freshly ground black
    pepper
2 pounds small Brussels sprouts, yellow
    leaves trimmed

2 tablespoons extra-virgin olive oil, plus
    more for drizzling
½ pound pancetta, cut into ½-inch cubes
3 fresh thyme sprigs, plus more for garnish
Four 7-ounce skinless black grouper,
    striped bass, or halibut fillets, about
    ¾ inch thick
2 tablespoons canola oil
Sweet smoked paprika

To prepare the lemon aïoli: In a small bowl, combine the mayonnaise, lemon juice, zest, garlic, and ¼ teaspoon each salt and pepper. Mix well. Transfer the aïoli to a tightly covered bowl or jar and refrigerate until ready to use. You can make this up to 3 days ahead.

Preheat the oven to 450°F.

Put the Brussels sprouts in a large mixing bowl. Add the olive oil, pancetta, and thyme; season with ¼ teaspoon salt and a pinch of pepper. Mix until the oil coats the sprouts.

Put a large ovenproof skillet over medium-high heat. Dump the Brussels sprout mixture into the hot skillet. Cook, stirring often, until the pancetta renders its fat and the sprouts start to brown, about 4 minutes.

Transfer the skillet to the oven and roast the sprouts, periodically shaking the pan or stirring with a large spoon to keep the pancetta from sticking and burning, until tender, roughly 15 minutes. Remove from the oven and cover to keep warm while you cook the fish.

Season the grouper on both sides with a fair amount of salt and pepper. Put a large skillet over medium-high heat and coat with the canola oil. When the oil is shimmering, carefully lay the fillets in the hot pan. Sear for 3 to 4 minutes without moving them around to help form a good sear and crust. Carefully flip the fish over and transfer the pan to the oven. Roast until cooked through, 3 to 4 minutes, until a fillet feels firm when you press it.

To serve, put the grouper in the center of 4 plates, drizzle with olive oil, scatter some lemon zest on top, and dust with paprika. Put a nice big pile of the Brussels sprouts on the side. Spoon the lemon aïoli into 4 small ramekins or bowls. Garnish with thyme sprigs.

PAN-ROASTED STRIPED BASS with tunisian chickpea salad and yogurt sauce

SERVES 4 ● This Mediterranean-inspired dish not only is light and healthy, but also has depth of flavor with a contrast of textures and temperatures. Most home cooks tell me they're intimidated by cooking fish with skin on; they find it tears or doesn't crisp up as it should. There are two keys to success: one is patience and the other is a well-seasoned cast-iron pan, preferably one that has gone through generations of use. The second alternative is to cheat and use a nonstick frying pan.

Two 15-ounce cans chickpeas, drained and rinsed

½ small red onion, finely chopped

½ English (hothouse) cucumber, cut lengthwise, seeded, and diced

¼ cup fresh cilantro leaves

2 celery stalks and leafy tops, chopped

¼ teaspoon ground cumin

¼ cup Tomato Harissa (page 243) or drained canned fire-roasted crushed tomatoes

½ cup extra-virgin olive oil

2 tablespoons champagne vinegar

Kosher salt and freshly ground black pepper

2 tablespoons canola oil

Four 8-ounce striped bass fillets, skin on, about 1½ inches thick

Yogurt Sauce (recipe follows)

Put ½ cup of the chickpeas in a mixing bowl. Mash the beans with a fork or potato masher until they are smashed but still have some texture. Add the remaining chickpeas, the onion, cucumber, cilantro, celery, cumin, harissa, olive oil, and vinegar; season generously with salt and pepper. Set aside at room temperature, or cover and refrigerate overnight. Return to room temperature before serving.

Preheat the oven to 450°F.

Put a large cast-iron skillet or nonstick ovenproof skillet over medium-high heat and coat with the canola oil. Pat both sides of the fish dry with paper

(recipe continues)

towels and season generously with salt and pepper. When the oil is shimmering, lay the fish skin side down in the pan. Sear for 4 to 5 minutes without moving the fillets. Transfer the pan to the oven and roast until the fish is opaque, 6 to 8 minutes. Remove the pan from the oven and carefully flip the fish over with a flat spatula, so the skin side is now up; it should be brown, crisp, and make a sound when you tap it. Let the fish sit in the hot pan for a minute to sear the bottom side.

To serve, pool 2 tablespoons of the yogurt sauce on each of 4 plates, place the fish skin side up on top of the sauce, and pile the chickpea salad next to it.

YOGURT SAUCE ● MAKES ½ CUP

½ cup Greek-style yogurt

Juice of ½ lemon

1 garlic clove, minced

1 tablespoon extra-virgin olive oil

Kosher salt and freshly ground black pepper

In a small bowl, combine the yogurt, lemon juice, garlic, and oil; season with salt and pepper. Transfer the yogurt sauce to a container, cover, and refrigerate until ready to use, for up to 7 days.

GRILLED TUNA STEAK with spring onions and provençal vinaigrette

SERVES 4 ● This might be the easiest recipe in the book and one you'll pull out over and over again for its ease and deliciousness. All you need are a few good ingredients and a hot grill. When it comes to buying fresh tuna, the species, or even the bright red color, is not necessarily an indicator of quality. In fact, fatty tuna, which is more desirable, is often paler but of no lesser quality. Fresh tuna is shiny, bright, and redolent of the ocean; it should talk to you. The Provençal vinaigrette is a full-flavored condiment you'll want to have on hand—always! Use it on everything from grilled fish to crostini and sandwiches. If you want to serve the tuna with another side dish, Sautéed Broccoli Rabe (page 192) is a good choice.

Four 8-ounce tuna steaks, 1 inch thick
3 tablespoons extra-virgin olive oil
Kosher salt and freshly ground black pepper

12 spring onions, white and green parts, tops trimmed
½ cup Provençal Vinaigrette (page 240)

Pat the tuna dry with paper towels and rub with 2 tablespoons of the oil. Sprinkle both sides of the tuna with a fair amount of salt and pepper—you should see the seasoning on the fish. Coat the onions in the remaining tablespoon of oil and season them with salt and pepper.

Preheat an outdoor gas or charcoal grill until very hot or put a grill pan or cast-iron skillet over medium-high heat. Lay the tuna steaks on the grill and sear for 2 to 3 minutes on each side, rotating halfway through cooking to "mark" them. As the tuna cooks, the red meat will become whiter; grill for a total of 5 to 6 minutes for medium-rare. A minute or two before the tuna is cooked, toss the spring onions on the grill and char them, turning often so they soften a bit but don't burn.

To serve, transfer the tuna to a cutting board and cut on a slight angle into 1-inch slices. Fan the pieces on 4 dinner plates, spoon the vinaigrette on top, and serve the spring onions on the side.

GRILLED WILD SALMON STEAK with fennel hash and sweet onion sauce

SERVES 4 ● Salmon steaks are shaped sort of like a horseshoe and have the bone left in the center. They're really thick and meaty and don't stick like fillets, which means they're perfect for the grill. Wild salmon is preferable to that raised in fish farms, as it tends to be healthier for you and taste better. Be sure to remove all the little pin bones with a pair of tweezers or have your fish guy do it.

With the bounty of produce on the planet, I gotta say onions are probably my favorite vegetable. They can be transformed in so many different ways. This onion sauce is so velvety you'd swear there is butter in it. The trick is to cook the onions low and slow so they don't brown or caramelize. This fennel hash is also killer with steak or eggs in the morning.

2 Yukon Gold potatoes (about 1 pound), peeled and cut into ½-inch cubes

Kosher salt and freshly ground black pepper

4 tablespoons canola oil

2 tablespoons unsalted butter

1 fennel bulb, top removed, fronds reserved, halved, cored, and cut into ½-inch dice

1 medium white onion, cut into ½-inch dice

2 garlic cloves, minced

Four 10-ounce wild salmon steaks, preferably sockeye, skin on, 1 to 1½ inches thick

1 tablespoon fennel seeds, toasted (see Note, page 52) and ground

1 cup Sweet Onion Sauce (recipe follows)

To prepare the hash: Put the potatoes in a pot, cover with cold water, and add 1 tablespoon salt. Bring to a boil over medium heat and cook for only 5 minutes; you want the potatoes to hold their shape and not cook all the way through, as they will continue to cook later. Drain and set aside.

Preheat an outdoor gas or charcoal grill until very hot, or put a grill pan over medium-high heat.

Put a large skillet over medium-high heat. Add 2 tablespoons of the oil and 1 tablespoon of the butter. When the butter is foamy, add the fennel and onion; season with salt and pepper. Cook, stirring, until the vegetables soften and start to get some color, about 7 minutes. Add the garlic and potatoes and crank the heat up to high. The potatoes will suck up a lot of oil, so add the remaining tablespoon butter now. Cook, gently stirring only occasionally, until the vegetables are soft and caramelized, 5 to 7 minutes.

Pat the salmon dry with paper towels and rub with the remaining 2 tablespoons oil. You'll make less smoke in your kitchen if you oil the fish and not the pan. Sprinkle both sides of the salmon with a fair amount of salt and pepper as well as the ground fennel. Lay the salmon steaks on the grill. Be patient—don't move the fish around. Instead, give it time to sear and form a crust, 2 to 3 minutes; the salmon will let you know when it is ready to be flipped because it won't stick to the grill. Flip and cook the other side for 2 to 3 minutes for medium-rare.

To serve, pool ¼ cup of the onion sauce on each of 4 plates, lay the fish on top, and spoon the hash on the side.

SWEET ONION SAUCE ● MAKES 2 CUPS

¼ cup plus 1 tablespoon extra-virgin
   olive oil
1 large Vidalia onion (about 1 pound),
   sliced
1 fresh thyme sprig

1 small bay leaf
Kosher salt and freshly ground black
   pepper
½ cup vegetable stock, plus more if
   needed

Put a pot over medium heat and coat with the 1 tablespoon oil. When the oil is hot, add the onion, thyme, and bay leaf; season with ½ teaspoon salt and ¼ teaspoon pepper. Cook and stir for 5 minutes, or until fragrant, but do not let the onion brown. Pour in the stock and bring to a simmer, then cover the pan and reduce the heat to low. Cook gently for 30 minutes, checking periodically to make sure the liquid has not completely evaporated and the onion is soupy; add a little stock if needed to keep the onion moist.

Remove the thyme and bay leaf. Transfer the onion to a blender and pulse until slightly chunky. Add the remaining ¼ cup oil and puree until the sauce is thick and creamy. Season with salt and pepper. The onion sauce can be cooled, covered, and refrigerated for up to 1 day. Reheat gently before serving.

STEAMED MUSSELS with tomato harissa broth and black sticky rice

SERVES 4 ● These are not your typical mussels served in run-of-the-mill white wine broth. The tomato harissa broth is an addictive elixir. Even though the mussels are served with rice, you will want to have plenty of crusty bread on hand to sop up the flavorful goodness.

1 cup black sticky rice

½ teaspoon kosher salt

2 pounds mussels

2 tablespoons extra-virgin olive oil

3 garlic cloves, minced

1½ cups dry white wine, such as
   Sauvignon Blanc

Tomato Harissa (page 243)

4 tablespoons (½ stick) unsalted butter

4 scallions, white and green parts, sliced
   diagonally

Cilantro leaves

INGREDIENT NOTE

black sticky rice

Also known as Thai black rice or purple sticky rice, this long-grain rice is a very attractive, deep purple color when cooked and has a sweet nutty flavor. Its firm texture and earthy taste mean it holds up well to assertive flavors. You can find it at Asian markets or online.

Put the rice in a small pot and add 1½ cups cold water and the salt. Bring to a boil over high heat. Reduce the heat to low, cover, and simmer until tender but still toothsome, 30 to 45 minutes. The cooking time for this rice varies; it's wise to check the instructions on the package.

Rinse the mussels under cold water while scrubbing with a vegetable brush. Remove any stringy mussel beards with your thumb and index finger as you wash them. Discard any mussels that are open or have broken shells.

Put a Dutch oven over medium heat and coat with the oil. Add the garlic and stir for 10 seconds. As soon as the garlic begins to brown, add the wine, mussels, and tomato harissa. Give everything a good toss. Cover the pot and crank up the heat to high. Steam the mussels for 5 minutes. Remove the cover, give the mussels a stir so all are in contact with the heat, and quickly put the lid back on. Steam for another 2 minutes. Stir in the butter to melt.

To serve, put about ½ cup rice in the center of each of 4 shallow bowls. Using tongs, fan the mussels around the rice and pour ½ cup of the broth over each portion. Garnish with the scallions and cilantro.

MAHOGANY BLACK COD with whipped parsnips, baby bok choy, and mustard sauce

SERVES 4 ● Beautiful plump fish covered with a butterscotch-colored sauce on a bed of snow-white puree, this is a very subtle dish, in a good way. The ratio of honey to mustard to soy sauce is perfect: you get sweet and salty with a little bite to complement the mild fish. The whipped parsnips are smooth and just rich enough with butter and cream. Bok choy makes a crisp accompaniment.

¼ cup honey

¼ cup Dijon mustard

1 tablespoon soy sauce

Four 7-ounce skinless black cod fillets,
   1 inch thick

3 parsnips (¾ pound), peeled and cut into
   1-inch pieces

3 medium Yukon Gold potatoes
   (1½ pounds), peeled and cut into 2-inch
   pieces

1 tablespoon kosher salt

Nonstick spray

¼ cup heavy cream

5 tablespoons unsalted butter, cut into
   cubes, at room temperature

4 heads baby bok choy, halved lengthwise

INGREDIENT NOTES

black cod

Black cod is actually not cod at all but sablefish. To add to the confusion, in some markets, the white fish is also referred to as butterfish, dubbed so for its rich creamy texture. Black cod is found all along the cold depths off the Pacific coast of the U.S. and Canada, with Alaskan fish considered the best in quality for its tender, sweet flavor. You'll often see smoked black cod in New York delis; the fish's high fat content makes it excellent for smoking. If you are landlocked and fresh sablefish/black cod is not available, check out the frozen section; the oily nature of the flesh stands up very well to freezing.

parsnips

Parsnips are a root vegetable that looks like a large white carrot. They have a sweet nutty flavor and a buttery-soft texture. Like potatoes, peeled parsnips will turn dark when exposed to the air, so cook them right away or hold them in water.

In a small bowl, blend the honey, mustard, and soy with a small whisk or dinner fork. Put the cod fillets in a resealable plastic bag and pour in half of the honey mustard. Reserve the remaining sauce for serving. Marinate the cod in the fridge for 6 hours or preferably overnight.

Put the parsnips and potatoes in a large pot and cover with cold water by 1 inch. Add the salt and bring to a boil over high heat. Once the water boils, reduce the heat to medium-low and simmer until the vegetables are very tender but not falling apart, about 30 minutes.

Meanwhile, preheat the oven to 450°F. Line a baking sheet with aluminum foil and coat with nonstick spray.

Drain the vegetables in a colander and transfer to a food processor. Puree, adding the cream and 4 tablespoons butter through the feed tube. Transfer to a medium pot, cover, and keep warm while you cook the fish.

Remove the fish from the marinade, scraping off the excess; discard the marinade. Lay the fillets in a single layer on the baking sheet. Bake until the fish flakes easily and is cooked through, 10 minutes.

While the fish is roasting, cook the bok choy. Arrange the bok choy cut side down in a single layer in a large skillet. Add ¼ cup water to coat the bottom of the pan and the remaining tablespoon of butter. Set over medium-high heat and cook, turning the bok choy with tongs, until the water and butter become a glaze and the bok choy has softened slightly, 5 minutes.

To serve, spoon the parsnip puree onto 4 plates, lay the fish on top, and arrange the bok choy next to it. Drizzle with the reserved honey mustard.

PAN-ROASTED HALF
BONELESS CHICKEN with
sautéed escarole

SERVES 4 ● This is one of those dishes where patronizing a local butcher, instead of a chain grocery store, will mean success. To halve and bone a couple of chickens is not an easy task, so leave this to the experts. Be specific with your butcher: request boneless chicken halves, meaning the first joint of the wing is clipped off and the only bone in the bird is the one that attaches the lower part of the wing to the breast, also known as an "airline." As an alternative, buy boneless chicken parts. There aren't a lot of ingredients to this dish; it really is all about the quality of chicken and a couple of well-seasoned cast-iron skillets. To get the super crispy skin, it is imperative that the chicken lies flat in the pan. Serve this with Roasted Garlic Mashed Potatoes (page 193) for a perfect Sunday supper.

Two 3-pound chickens, halved and boned,
 skin on, or 3 pounds boneless chicken
 parts, skin on, preferably free-range
Kosher salt and freshly ground black
 pepper
¼ cup canola oil
2 heads escarole (about 1½ pounds;
 see Note, page 106)

¼ cup extra-virgin olive oil
4 garlic cloves, minced
¼ cup dry white wine, such as Sauvignon
 Blanc
2 tablespoons unsalted butter
1 tablespoon chopped fresh flat-leaf
 parsley

Preheat the oven to 450°F.

Place two cast-iron or heavy-bottomed ovenproof skillets over high heat; cast iron will yield a crispier skin. Season the chickens generously with salt and pepper; you should see the seasoning on the meat. Coat each pan with 2 tablespoons of canola oil. Once the oil is shimmering, lay the chicken halves in the pans, skin side down. It's super important to make sure the chicken lies flat and all of the skin is in contact with the pan. Cook until the skin starts to brown, 3 to 5 minutes. Do not move the chicken or the skin will tear. Transfer the pans to the oven and roast until the juices run clear when the meat is pierced with a knife, about 20 minutes.

Meanwhile, cut the escarole lengthwise through the core and then crosswise into ½-inch-wide strips. Put the escarole in a large bowl of water. Swish the water around; sand will fall to the bottom of the bowl. Lift the escarole out with your hands and put it on a kitchen towel to dry; you should have about 5 quarts of escarole. It might seem like a lot, but trust me, it cooks down dramatically.

Put a large pot or skillet over medium heat and coat with the olive oil. When the oil is shimmering, add the garlic and cook, stirring, until golden, about 30 seconds. Raise the heat to high and add several handfuls of the escarole, stirring to coat with the oil. Cook, stirring occasionally, until the escarole starts to wilt. When there is more room in the pan, add the rest of the escarole. Cook until most of the liquid is evaporated, about 5 minutes. Season with salt and pepper.

Transfer the chicken to a warm platter, skin side up. To make a quick pan sauce, pour out the excess fat from the pan drippings. Place the pans over two burners set on medium-high heat. Add 2 tablespoons wine to each pan. Using a wooden spoon, scrape up the brown bits stuck to the bottom of the pan. Add 1 tablespoon butter to each, stirring to melt, and sprinkle with parsley.

To serve, divide the escarole among 4 plates and lay half a roasted chicken on top, skin side up. Drizzle the pan sauce on top.

WHOLE ROASTED CHICKEN
with plumped raisins, toasted pine nuts, and arugula

SERVES 2 TO 4 ● Succulent, tender, and aromatic, roast chicken is a dish that all cooks should have in their arsenal. There are many schools of thought on how to master the perfect roast chicken. My philosophy is the simpler the better. I don't use a big roasting pan or rack, truss the bird, or change the oven temperature fifty times. As far as technique goes, I like to start roasting the chicken breast side down to protect it from drying out in the initial intense heat. Gravity also works on your side that way; all of the juices gather in the breast meat during the first half of cooking, keeping the meat really moist. Then I turn the bird over to finish cooking and brown the breast. Swiss Chard and Caramelized Onion Panade (page 183) makes a terrific side.

⅓ cup raisins

½ cup extra-virgin olive oil

¼ fresh rosemary sprig

One 3½-pound whole chicken, preferably free-range

4 fresh thyme sprigs

Kosher salt and freshly ground black pepper

1½ teaspoons canola oil

¼ cup dry white wine, such as Sauvignon Blanc

2 cups fresh arugula leaves, stemmed

2 tablespoons pine nuts, toasted (see Note, page 54)

Preheat the oven to 300°F.

Put the raisins in a small ramekin and pour in the olive oil and 1 tablespoon water. Add the rosemary. Cover with aluminum foil and bake for 30 minutes, or until the raisins are plump. Remove the raisins from the oven and set aside to cool.

Crank the oven temperature up to 450°F.

Remove the neck and giblets from the cavity and rinse the chicken inside and out under cold water. Pat dry thoroughly with paper towels. Run your

(recipe continues)

finger between the skin and the breast meat of the chicken, and slip the thyme sprigs in there. Season the body and cavity of the chicken generously with salt and pepper.

Put a 10-inch ovenproof skillet over medium-high heat and add the canola oil. When the oil is hot, lay the chicken in the pan, breast side down, tucking the wings under. Put the skillet in the oven and roast until the chicken starts to brown, about 35 minutes.

Carefully take the pan out of the oven. Insert tongs or a sturdy wooden spoon into the cavity of the chicken and gently lift the chicken out, being careful not to tear the skin. Tilt the chicken slightly so all of the juices from the inside run out into the pan. Set the chicken on a large plate for a minute. Discard all of the pan juices, which will mostly be fat. Nestle the chicken back in the pan, breast side up. Return it to the oven and roast for 30 minutes. The chicken is done when the juices run clear when the meat is pierced with a knife. To be extra sure, pop an instant-read thermometer into the thickest part of the thigh; it should read 165°F. Transfer the chicken to a cutting board and let rest for 5 minutes before carving so the juices can settle back into the meat.

To make a quick pan sauce, pour off the excess fat from the pan drippings. Put the skillet over medium-high heat and add the wine. Using a wooden spoon, scrape up the brown bits stuck to bottom of the pan. Season with salt and pepper.

To serve, put a bed of arugula on individual plates or on a platter and arrange the carved chicken on top. Scatter the raisins and pine nuts all over. Drizzle with the pan sauce and a little of the raisin oil.

CURRIED LENTIL STEW
with greek yogurt

SERVES 4 ● This hearty vegetarian stew has special memories for me. I used to make it almost every day when I was broke, back when I was trying to open my first restaurant. And yet I never get tired of it. This dish has layers of flavors, comes together pretty rapidly, and leaves you fully satisfied.

4 tablespoons canola oil

1 carrot, diced

2 celery stalks, diced

2 cups lentils

1 bay leaf

1 tablespoon curry powder

1 teaspoon red curry paste

1 teaspoon ground cumin

1 large white onion, cut into ½-inch
   wedges

Kosher salt and freshly ground black
   pepper

2 tablespoons honey

2 tablespoons unseasoned rice vinegar

1 head kale (about ¾ pound), cut into
   1-inch pieces

¼ cup Greek-style yogurt

¼ cup roasted and salted cashews,
   coarsely chopped

Fresh cilantro leaves

Put a large pot over medium heat and add 2 tablespoons of the oil. When the oil is shimmering, add the carrot and celery. Cook and stir until the vegetables soften a bit, 3 to 4 minutes. Add the lentils, bay leaf, curry powder, curry paste, and cumin and cook until the lentils are coated and the spices are fragrant, 2 to 3 minutes. Add 1 quart water, increase the heat to high, and bring to a boil. Reduce the heat to low, cover, and simmer until the lentils are tender and the water is absorbed, 20 to 30 minutes.

Set a large skillet over medium-high heat and add the remaining 2 table-spoons oil. When the oil is shimmering, add the onion. Cook, stirring occasionally, until the onion is soft and caramelized, 8 to 10 minutes. Season with salt and pepper. Reduce the heat to medium, add the honey, and cook until the onion is brown and sticky, 2 to 3 minutes. Add the vinegar and kale. Fold the kale over so it comes in contact with the bottom of the pan and wilts, 2 to 3 minutes; the kale will not be fully cooked at this point.

Mix the kale mixture into the lentils. Simmer over low heat until the stew is thick, 5 to 8 minutes. Serve the lentil stew in bowls, garnishing each with a dollop of yogurt, some cashews, and a few cilantro leaves.

MUSTARD AND MOLASSES
ST. LOUIS RIBS
with celery root slaw

SERVES 4 ● When it comes to pork ribs, for my money I prefer St. Louis ribs to baby back. They're long and thin with a good amount of meat, not to mention less expensive. Grilling the ribs to crisp them up after they have slow-roasted for a couple of hours may require a little extra effort, but believe me, you'll reap the rewards with insanely tasty ribs that will have everyone licking their fingers. A creamy cool slaw and sweet-rich barbecue sauce round out this comfort-food meal.

2 racks St. Louis pork ribs (about
   4½ pounds)
¼ cup whole-grain mustard
1 tablespoon Dijon mustard
¼ cup molasses
1 tablespoon white vinegar

2 teaspoons kosher salt
1 teaspoon freshly ground black pepper
Canola oil, for brushing the grill
Killer Barbecue Sauce (page 245)
Celery Root Slaw (recipe follows)

To prepare the ribs, start by removing the thin layer of skin from the underside of the ribs. Lay the racks down so the ribs curve up on the ends. With a sharp knife, gently cut under the membrane on one corner until you have enough to grab. Now, take a paper towel and gently pull back the skin. With any luck you should be able to get most of it off in a single shot. Cut the racks in half so they are easier to work with.

In a small bowl, combine the mustards, molasses, vinegar, salt, and pepper. Put the ribs side by side in a large roasting pan. Rub or brush the mustard and molasses mixture all over them. Cover the pan tightly with aluminum foil and refrigerate for 12 to 24 hours.

Preheat the oven to 300°F. Remove the ribs from the fridge and set on the counter while the oven is heating.

Put the ribs in the oven and cook, covered, until very tender, about 2 hours. Remove from the oven, uncover, and cool to room temperature. The ribs can be covered and refrigerated for a day or two at this point.

Preheat an outdoor grill or a grill pan to medium-high heat. Rub the grill with oil to prevent sticking. Put the ribs on the grill and cook, turning once, until they begin to brown and get crusty, about 3 minutes (longer if the ribs are coming straight from the fridge). Brush the ribs with some of the barbecue sauce and grill until the sauce caramelizes, 2 minutes. Turn the ribs over, brush with more sauce, and grill for 2 minutes.

Transfer the ribs to a platter and serve with the celery root slaw and more barbecue sauce on the side.

CELERY ROOT SLAW ● MAKES 5 CUPS

1 celery root (about 1½ pounds; see Note), peeled and cut into matchsticks

1 carrot, cut into matchsticks

½ small red onion, thinly sliced

½ cup fresh parsley leaves, coarsely chopped

½ cup Best Mayonnaise (page 246) or quality store-bought mayo

¼ cup sour cream

Juice of ½ lemon

1 tablespoon Dijon mustard

1 teaspoon kosher salt

½ teaspoon freshly ground black pepper

INGREDIENT NOTE

celery root

Let's be frank: celery root (also called celeriac) is not the prettiest vegetable on the planet; it looks a bit gnarly with a lot of bumps and little knobby roots at the bottom. But underneath the disguise lies a delicious surprise—a flavor similar to that of celery, but a little milder, rounder, and nuttier. Its flesh is smooth and dense, a bit like a firm potato. It is terrific raw or cooked and mashed, like other winter root vegetables. For this recipe, the celery root can be thinly sliced by hand or on a mandoline. As a last resort, grate it on a box grater.

In a large bowl, combine the celery root, carrot, onion, and parsley. Add the mayonnaise, sour cream, lemon juice, mustard, salt, and pepper. Toss the slaw until the ingredients are well blended. Feel free to make the slaw an hour or two in advance; the flavor gets better as it sits.

SLOW-ROASTED BONELESS SHORT RIBS with romesco sauce

SERVES 4 ● Beef short ribs are commonly braised for hours. What is slightly unusual and great about this recipe is that the short ribs are slow-roasted until tender and then grilled to impart a smoky char. It may seem like a difficult recipe, but I swear it's not, and the delicious result is so worth the time. The ribs need a day to marinate, so plan accordingly. After tasting this dish, you'll never braise a short rib again! Use any leftover meat to make Short Rib and Fontina Cheese Panini with Tomato-Onion Chutney (page 120) or Pappardelle with Beef Sugo and Ricotta (page 111). This is a really rich dish; all it needs to round it out is a simple green salad.

To make the spiced short ribs really sing, I prepare a version of Spanish romesco sauce. Bold, tangy, and definitely habit-forming, romesco looks ordinary enough but in one bite transforms the dish. When making the sauce, it's important to use a food processor and not a blender so it retains a chunky texture. This recipe will make more than you need for the short ribs and is a terrific go-to sauce to keep around. Try it with grilled vegetables and seafood (it's particularly awesome with shrimp), tossed with pasta, or as a sandwich spread.

2 tablespoons sweet smoked paprika

2 tablespoons ground ginger

2 tablespoons chili powder

3 garlic cloves, minced

¼ cup canola oil

Kosher salt and freshly ground black
  pepper

6 pounds boneless beef short ribs

1 tablespoon extra-virgin olive oil, plus
  more for drizzling

3 cups assorted mixed greens

1 teaspoon freshly squeezed lemon juice

½ cup Romesco Sauce (recipe follows)

2 tablespoons skinned hazelnuts, toasted
  (see Note, page 54) and chopped

2 tablespoons whole almonds, toasted
  (see Note, page 54), and chopped

1 lemon, cut into wedges

(recipe continues)

In a small bowl, combine the paprika, ginger, chili powder, garlic, canola oil, and 1 tablespoon each of salt and pepper; stir thoroughly to combine. Rub the spice mixture all over the short ribs to evenly coat the meat. Transfer the ribs to a large resealable plastic bag and refrigerate for 12 to 24 hours.

Preheat the oven to 300°F.

Arrange the short ribs on a wire rack set on top of a baking pan. Bake for 1½ hours, to render the fat. Remove the ribs and the rack, discard the fat, and return the ribs to the pan (without the rack). Cover with foil and bake until tender, about 1½ hours. Allow the ribs to cool to room temperature, then cover and chill completely in the fridge for at least 1 hour. All of this can be knocked out a day or two in advance.

Preheat an outdoor grill or a grill pan to medium-high heat. Cut the ribs against the grain into 1-inch strips, reserving the scraps. Drizzle the ribs with olive oil. Working in batches, grill the cut side of the ribs for 2 to 3 minutes on each side, until nicely charred.

In a mixing bowl, toss the salad greens with the olive oil and lemon juice and season with salt and pepper.

To serve, divide the ribs among 4 plates and arrange a handful of salad greens next to them. Spoon the romesco sauce over the meat, sprinkle with the nuts, and garnish with lemon wedges.

ROMESCO SAUCE ● MAKES ABOUT 2¾ CUPS

1 cup ½-inch cubes sourdough bread

1 cup plus 1 tablespoon extra-virgin
  olive oil

½ white onion, thinly sliced (1 cup)

Kosher salt and freshly ground black
  pepper

2 jarred roasted red bell peppers,
  rinsed

¼ cup sherry vinegar

1 tablespoon freshly squeezed lemon
  juice

2 tablespoons tomato paste

3 garlic cloves, coarsely chopped

¼ cup blanched hazelnuts, toasted
  (see Note, page 54) and chopped

¼ cup whole almonds, toasted (see
  Note, page 54) and chopped

Preheat the oven to 350°F.

Put the bread cubes on a baking sheet. Bake until lightly toasted, roughly 10 minutes.

Put a skillet over medium heat and coat with the 1 tablespoon oil. When the oil is hot, add the onion and season with salt and pepper. Cook, stirring, until the onion is caramelized, about 8 minutes. Remove from the heat and set aside to cool to room temperature.

In a food processor, combine the red peppers with the vinegar, lemon juice, tomato paste, and garlic. Process for 10 to 15 seconds until smooth. Add the croutons and the nuts; process for another 10 to 15 seconds until thick. With the processor running, slowly drizzle in the remaining 1 cup oil until incorporated. If the sauce is too thick for your liking, add water, a tablespoon at a time, and pulse a couple of times to combine. Season the sauce with salt and pepper. Refrigerate until ready to use, for up to 3 days. Bring to room temperature before serving.

FRIED "BUFFALO STYLE" RABBIT with blue cheese and hot sauce

SERVES 4 ● Rabbit is a great change of pace from the everyday and luckily is becoming more widely available. Have your butcher cut up the rabbit for you; it can be tricky to do at home. The flavor is mild and the meat tender; you'll swear it tastes like chicken. The hot sauce and blue cheese do not overwhelm; they actually bring out the flavor of the rabbit. The blue cheese sauce also makes a great salad dressing, thinned with a tablespoon of water.

1 yellow onion, halved

1 garlic clove, smashed

½ bunch fresh flat-leaf parsley

2 bay leaves

1 fresh thyme sprig

Kosher salt and freshly ground black pepper

1 teaspoon whole black peppercorns

Two 3-pound rabbits, each cut into 8 pieces, rinsed

1 quart buttermilk

1 tablespoon Habañero Hot Sauce (page 244) or store-bought hot sauce, such as Tabasco, plus more for serving

3 cups all-purpose flour

1 tablespoon garlic powder

2 teaspoons sweet smoked paprika

Canola oil, for deep-frying

Blue Cheese Sauce (recipe follows)

Fill a large pot with water and add the onion, garlic, parsley, bay leaves, thyme, 2 tablespoons salt, and the peppercorns. Bring to a rapid boil and cook for 5 minutes to infuse the water with the aromatics. Add the rabbit and bring back up to a boil; this should take roughly 5 minutes. Strain the rabbit pieces, transfer to a baking dish, and set aside to cool to room temperature.

Pour the buttermilk over the rabbit, turning the pieces so they are well coated. Add the hot sauce. Cover with plastic wrap and refrigerate for at least 6 hours. If you have the time, marinate the rabbit for up to 2 days—the buttermilk tenderizes the meat.

Spread the flour on a large shallow platter. Add the garlic powder and paprika; season with lots of salt and pepper. Mix the seasoned flour with your fingers until all the ingredients are thoroughly incorporated. Remove the rabbit pieces from the buttermilk, discarding the buttermilk. Roll the pieces in the flour, a few at a time, until well coated, tapping off the excess. Let the rabbit sit in the flour and dry out while you heat the oil; this will help the crust stay on better. The buttermilk will keep absorbing the seasoned flour, which then fries up to form a crunchy crust.

Heat 3 inches of oil to 375°F in a countertop electric fryer or deep pot. (I like to start with very hot oil because as soon as the rabbit is added, the temperature drops significantly.) If you don't have a deep-fry thermometer, a good way to test if the oil is hot enough is to stick the end of a wooden spoon or chopstick in it. If bubbles circle around the end, then you're good to go.

Working in batches, carefully add 3 or 4 pieces of rabbit at a time. Fry until the rabbit is golden and crisp with even color, turning halfway through cooking, about 10 minutes total. Transfer to a platter lined with paper towels and repeat with the remaining rabbit pieces.

To serve, arrange the fried rabbit on a large platter. Serve with hot sauce and the blue cheese sauce on the side for dipping.

BLUE CHEESE SAUCE ● MAKES 1½ CUPS

1 cup sour cream
1 cup crumbled Danish blue cheese
2 tablespoons buttermilk

Kosher salt and freshly ground black pepper

In a small bowl, combine the sour cream, cheese, and buttermilk; season with salt and pepper. Mash the ingredients with a fork; the sauce should remain somewhat lumpy.

EXTRA-LARGE PLATES

Family recipes, those passed down through the generations, carry forward a flavor of heritage and identity. You know how to make them and everyone knows how to eat them. To me, these are the classic foods that are a part of family traditions: hearty, impressive dishes that excite oohs and aahs when you ceremoniously present them in the middle of the table.

The straightforward, accessible recipes in this chapter are big centerpiece dishes, powered with all of the elements to complete the meal, like sauces and sides. Some are one-pot wonders; others have a couple of components that may take some time to make, but are worth every minute. So too is the loving act of sharing them. Whether for a holiday or special occasion, these family-style suppers are worthy of bringing people together. Going beyond custom or tradition, they simply taste like home.

BRAISED CHICKEN with apricots, green olives, and herbed couscous

SERVES 6 ● A departure from classic chicken stew, this one-pot wonder with Middle Eastern flair is a little bit exotic but not off-putting or difficult to make in the slightest. In fact, my kids love it. The sweet apricots and salty olives play nicely off each other and collide under a shower of cilantro to jack up the flavor even more. The recipe *should* make a little extra for leftovers, which are even better the next day.

½ cup all-purpose flour

4 pounds chicken thighs (about 12), bone in, skin on, preferably free-range

Kosher salt and freshly ground black pepper

¼ cup canola oil

2 carrots, cut into large chunks

1 medium white onion, cut into large dice

3 celery stalks, cut into large chunks

1 teaspoon ground cinnamon

1 cup dried apricots (about 20)

1½ cups pitted green olives, such as Manzanilla

3 cups chicken stock

1 cup orange juice

1 cup couscous

6 scallions, white and light green parts, sliced

1 cup fresh cilantro leaves, coarsely chopped

2 tablespoons coarsely chopped fresh mint leaves

3 tablespoons unsalted butter

Preheat the oven to 375°F.

Spread the flour in a large shallow plate. Season the chicken liberally with salt and pepper. Dredge the chicken lightly in the flour to coat all sides, tapping off the excess. Put a Dutch oven or large ovenproof pot over high heat and coat with the oil. When the oil is shimmering, add 5 pieces of chicken and brown them for 4 to 6 minutes on each side, without moving them around too much so you get a good sear. Transfer the chicken to a platter and repeat with the remaining thighs.

To the drippings in the pot, add the carrots, onion, and celery. Cook, stirring, for about 5 minutes, or until the vegetables soften and begin to get some color. Add 2 teaspoons salt, 1 teaspoon pepper, the cinnamon, apricots, olives, and stock. Nestle the chicken in the pot so the thighs are covered with apricots, olives, and stock. Pour any drippings collected from the platter into the pot. Bring the stew to a boil, then cover and transfer to the oven. Bake for 1 hour, or until your kitchen smells amazing.

Combine the orange juice, ½ cup water, and 1 tablespoon salt in a small pot over high heat and bring to a boil. Remove from the heat, stir in the couscous, and quickly cover to keep in the heat. Let stand for 10 minutes, until the couscous is soft.

Combine the scallions, cilantro, and mint in a small bowl.

Remove the chicken from the oven and gently stir in the butter until completely melted.

To serve, put the couscous in a serving bowl and fluff with a fork. Fold in half of the scallion mixture. Sprinkle the remaining scallion mixture over the braised chicken, and serve it right out of the pot.

SLOW-ROASTED PORK SHOULDER with pickled onions

SERVES 8 ● Sweet, succulent, and aromatic, this sophisticated yet homey family-style supper is definitely one to pull out when company is coming. Not only is pork shoulder super satisfying, but the cut is also an inexpensive way to feed a lot of people. Serve with herbaceous Parsley Sauce (page 239) and creamy Cheese Grits (page 189) for a lethal combination.

2 tablespoons canola oil

1 large fennel bulb, top removed, halved, cored, and thinly sliced

1 large onion, halved and thinly sliced

¼ cup fennel seeds

1 tablespoon coriander seeds

1 tablespoon red pepper flakes

1 tablespoon chili powder

1 tablespoon ground cinnamon

¼ cup kosher salt

1 tablespoon freshly ground black pepper

1 boneless pork shoulder (about 5 pounds), trimmed of excess fat

Pickled onions (page 235)

Put a large skillet over medium heat and coat with the oil. When the oil is hot, add the fennel and onion. Cook and stir for 10 minutes, until the vegetables are soft. Remove from the heat and set aside to cool.

In a mortar and pestle or spice grinder, combine the fennel seeds, coriander, red pepper flakes, chili powder, and cinnamon. Mash or buzz until you have a spice powder. Put the spice powder in a small bowl and mix in the salt and pepper.

Put the pork, fat side up, in a roasting pan. Using a sharp knife, make small slits all over the surface of the meat. Rub the spice mixture all over the pork, inside and out, being sure to get in the incisions. Lift up the top flap and spoon the fennel and onion mixture inside the pork.

Preheat the oven to 300°F.

Pour in just enough water to film the bottom of the roasting pan. Cover the pan tightly with aluminum foil. Slow-roast the pork for 2 hours.

Increase the oven temperature to 425°F and roast for another hour, until the meat is falling apart. Carefully transfer the pork to a serving platter, tent with foil, and allow to rest for 10 minutes. Serve the pork with some pickled onions on top, and chow down!

GRILLED LEG OF LAMB with salsa verde

SERVES 6 TO 8 ● Bone-in leg of lamb has marvelous flavor and is a traditional roast for festive family gatherings. There is a great deal of versatility in this cut, but my favorite way to prepare it is on a grill. Slow cooking on a grill keeps the lamb really tender and moist while adding an awesome smoky taste. The yogurt and lemon marinade helps carry the deep flavors of the lamb and also gives the meat a nice crust. The lamb needs to marinate for several hours, so plan accordingly. I love this with Greek Farro Salad (page 79), a bright, refreshing complement to the charred lamb.

One 6-pound leg of lamb, bone in, trimmed of excess fat
½ cup Greek-style yogurt
6 garlic cloves, minced
2 tablespoons finely chopped fresh rosemary
Juice of 1 lemon

2 tablespoons extra-virgin olive oil, plus more for the grill
1 tablespoon kosher salt
1 tablespoon freshly ground black pepper
3 lemons, halved
Salsa Verde (recipe follows)

NOTE

carving a leg of lamb

A leg of lamb is one of simplest roasts to carve. There are no complicated techniques involved and the only tools required are a sharp knife and a cutting board. Hold the leg bone securely with a clean kitchen towel and lift it up slightly so the leg is tilted. Slice the rounded side of the meat into thin pieces until you hit the bone. Turn the leg over so it sits steady on the board and carve the other side in the same manner. To make the most tender slices, always cut across the grain of the meat, which radiates outward from the bone.

Put the lamb in a large roasting pan and pat dry with paper towels.

In a small bowl, combine the yogurt, garlic, rosemary, lemon juice, oil, salt, and pepper and mix well. Using your hands, rub the paste all over the lamb. Cover with plastic wrap and marinate in the refrigerator, turning occasionally, for at least 6 hours or, even better, overnight.

(recipe continues)

Preheat an outdoor gas grill until very hot. Rub the grill grates with oil to prevent sticking. Put the lamb on the grill, reduce the heat to the lowest setting, and close the cover. Grill the lamb, turning periodically, until a meat thermometer inserted into the center of the lamb registers about 135°F (be careful that the thermometer does not touch the bone), about 1¼ hours. Transfer the lamb to a cutting board and allow to rest for 10 minutes before carving. The internal temperature will continue to rise 5 to 10 degrees.

Right before serving, put the lemon halves, cut side down, on the grill and char for 1 minute—you won't believe how much juice you get.

Carve the lamb and serve drizzled with salsa verde and a lemon half for a good squeeze of lemon juice.

A RAINY-DAY METHOD

Prepare the lamb as above, but roast in a roasting pan in a preheated 325°F oven for 1½ to 2 hours for medium-rare.

SALSA VERDE ● MAKES ¾ CUP

1 cup firmly packed fresh flat-leaf
  parsley leaves, chopped
3 tablespoons capers, drained, rinsed,
  and chopped
2 anchovies in oil, drained and finely
  chopped
2 garlic cloves, minced

½ shallot, chopped
Finely grated zest of 1 lemon
½ teaspoon freshly ground black
  pepper
Pinch of red pepper flakes
½ cup extra-virgin olive oil

In a small bowl, combine all the ingredients, mixing well with a spoon.

ALMOND BRAISED LAMB SHANKS with toasted almond salad

SERVES 6 ● This out-of-the-ordinary stew is seriously good and its enticing aroma seductive. The sauce is smooth and complex: cinnamon, mustard, cumin, fenugreek, and cardamom all add up to an intriguing flavor that really lingers. The parsley-almond garnish adds brightness to the dish. Sweet, nutty, and crunchy, with layers of Indian spices, this killer recipe is a must-try. Serve it over basmati rice.

2 cups sliced almonds (7½ ounces)

6 cardamom pods

1 star anise

1 tablespoon fenugreek

1 tablespoon mustard seeds

1 tablespoon cumin seeds

1 cinnamon stick

1 large onion, coarsely chopped

6 garlic cloves, coarsely chopped

One 1-inch piece fresh ginger, peeled and coarsely chopped

1 bunch fresh cilantro, coarsely chopped

¼ cup tomato paste

2 cups plain yogurt

Two 12-ounce bottles amber beer, such as Bass

Kosher salt and freshly ground black pepper

1 cup all-purpose flour

Six 1-pound lamb shanks

¼ cup canola oil

Toasted Almond Salad (recipe follows)

Preheat the oven to 325°F.

Toast the almonds, cardamom, anise, fenugreek, mustard and cumin seeds, and cinnamon in a dry large skillet over low heat; be sure to shake the pan so they don't scorch. When the almonds and spices smell fragrant, not burnt, they're done. Because of the volume of nuts and spices, this can take about 5 minutes. Remove from the heat and let cool slightly.

Transfer the mixture to a blender. Blend on high speed to grind everything up. Add the onion, garlic, ginger, cilantro, tomato paste, and 1 cup water. Blend again, holding down the lid, until the vegetables and cilantro are chopped up. Pour the mixture into a large bowl, stir in the yogurt and the beer, and season with salt and pepper.

Spread the flour in a large shallow platter; season with 1 teaspoon salt and ½ teaspoon pepper. Mix together until the seasonings are thoroughly incorporated. Dredge the lamb shanks in the flour, tapping off the excess.

Put a Dutch oven or large ovenproof pot over medium-high heat and coat with the oil. When the oil is shimmering, add the lamb shanks in batches, turning with tongs every few minutes until they are golden brown on all sides, about 15 minutes total. Transfer the shanks to a baking sheet as they are done. Be sure the oil and leftover flour in the pan hasn't turned black; if so wipe out the pot.

Return the seared shanks to the pot, trying to get them in a single layer as best you can. Pour in any accumulated juices and the spice mixture so the shanks are completely submerged; if they aren't, add water to cover. Cover with a lid or aluminum foil and braise in the oven, basting and turning occasionally, until the lamb is tender and falling off the bone, about 2½ hours.

Transfer the shanks to a baking sheet. Pour the braising liquid through a strainer into a large bowl, pressing on the solids with the back of a spoon. Return the strained liquid to the pot and simmer over medium heat for 2 to 3 minutes. Nestle the lamb shanks back in the pot, basting with the sauce. Simmer for another minute or two, until the sauce coats the back of the spoon.

Serve the lamb topped with some of the sauce and flanked by a few handfuls of the salad.

TOASTED ALMOND SALAD ● MAKES 4 CUPS, LIGHTLY PACKED

2 cups bitter greens, such as radicchio and endive, cut into thin ribbons
1 cup fresh parsley leaves, coarsely chopped
1 cup sliced almonds, toasted (see Note, page 54)
1 lemon, halved
¼ cup extra-virgin olive oil
Kosher salt and freshly ground pepper

Combine the greens, parsley, and almonds in a mixing bowl. Squeeze the lemon over the salad, squeezing through your fingers to catch the seeds. Drizzle with the oil and season with salt and pepper. Toss gently.

THYME-SMOKED FOUR-INCH PORTERHOUSE STEAK

SERVES 6 TO 8 ● So you feel like steak? This one is a monster! For all of the card-carrying carnivores out there, this dish will turn you on. Porterhouse is a great cut because it's like two for one—on one side of the steak you have the tender filet and on the other, the firm New York strip. Grilling with wood chips is a common way to infuse flavor into meat, but for extra oomph, I turn to herb-infused smoke instead. Tossing damp woody herbs like thyme (rosemary would work here as well) directly onto the fire lends a distinctive earthy essence. The intoxicating smell makes your belly grumble and always has a "wow factor" with guests. Serve with Roasted Garlic (page 238) and/or Porcini Worcestershire Sauce (page 242).

One 3- to 4-pound porterhouse steak, 3 to 4 inches thick
1 big bunch (¼ pound) fresh thyme
2 tablespoons kosher salt

1 tablespoon freshly ground black pepper
1 tablespoon extra-virgin olive oil, plus more for the grill

Let the steak stand at room temperature for 30 minutes. Take 6 sprigs of the thyme and strip the leaves from the stems. Finely chop the leaves; you should have about 1 tablespoon. Set aside. Put half of the remaining thyme sprigs in a small bowl. Cover with cool water and soak for 10 minutes while heating the grill.

Preheat a gas or charcoal grill to medium-low. Pat the steak dry and rub both sides with the chopped thyme, salt, and pepper, pressing to adhere. Drizzle both sides of the steak with the oil and rub the grill grates with oil to prevent sticking. Put the steak on the grill, close the lid, and grill for 8 minutes for medium-rare. Open the lid and, using tongs, carefully lift up the grill grate and toss half of the soaked thyme sprigs directly onto the gas burner or coals so they smolder, imparting an amazing aroma and flavor. Rotate the steak a quarter turn to "mark" it. Close the lid and cook the steak for another 8 minutes. Open the lid and again, carefully lift up the grill grate and set the remaining soaked thyme directly on the fire. Turn over the steak and cook for 8 minutes, rotate, and cook for 8 minutes more. Check the internal temperature of the steak with an instant-read thermometer; it should be about 125°F for medium-rare.

Transfer the steak to a cutting board and allow to rest for 10 minutes so the juices can settle before carving.

To serve, cut the meat away from the bone and set the bone on a serving platter. Cut the steak into ¼-inch-thick slices. Shingle the slices around the bone. Scatter the remaining thyme sprigs on top.

PORK LOIN stuffed with dried cherries and swiss chard

SERVES 8 TO 10 ● Pork loin is always welcome at any family table or dinner party, and thankfully it turns out to be as easy to make as it is impressive. Assemble it a day or two in advance and just pop the pork in the oven before dinner. The colorful jewel tones of the stuffing make this dish look as good as it tastes. Once you have the basic technique down, you can change the stuffing any number of ways—use different kinds of bread, dried fruit, wine, herbs.

½ cup dried cherries

½ cup fruity red wine, such as Pinot Noir

1 bunch Swiss chard (about ¾ pound)

2 tablespoons extra-virgin olive oil

½ large white onion, thinly sliced

Kosher salt and freshly ground black
  pepper

2 garlic cloves, chopped

One 5-pound pork loin, rinsed and patted
  dry with paper towels

2 tablespoons plain dried bread crumbs

2 tablespoons chopped fresh rosemary

½ cup chicken stock

Put the dried cherries in a bowl. Heat the wine in a small pot or in the microwave and pour over the cherries. Cover with plastic wrap and allow to sit and plump up for about 20 minutes.

Cut the ribs out of the Swiss chard and set aside. Roll the leaves into a bundle and coarsely chop into 1-inch ribbons; you should have about 8 cups. Put the chopped chard in a colander and rinse well. Set aside to drain. Cut the ribs crosswise into ¼-inch pieces. (Why do people throw them away? They give a little crunch and added texture.)

Preheat the oven to 425°F.

Put a large pot over high heat and coat with the oil. When the oil is hot, add the chard ribs and onion; season with salt and pepper. Cook and stir with a wooden spoon until the vegetables soften, about 4 minutes. Once they're cooked down, add the garlic and give it a stir; cook for a minute until fragrant. Add the chard leaves. Turn the leaves over until the chard releases its moisture and cooks down, about 3 minutes. Season again with a pinch each of salt and pepper. If you want to stuff the loin immediately, spread the chard mixture out on a baking sheet to cool quickly; if you've got the time, simply turn off the heat and let it cool in the pot.

Using a sharp knife, cut the pork loin lengthwise down the middle—do not cut all the way through to the other side—and open it up flat like a book. Season the surface of the pork generously with salt and pepper. Evenly distribute the cooled stuffing on the bottom half of the pork. Sprinkle the bread crumbs on top of the chard to soak up any extra juices. Drain the wine from the cherries and reserve. Distribute the macerated cherries evenly on top and pat down. Carefully fold the top of the pork loin over; just push the stuffing back in if it starts to come out.

Cut kitchen twine into six 12-inch pieces. Tie the roast securely with the string at intervals to hold it together (but not so tight that you squeeze out the stuffing). Scatter half of the rosemary evenly on top of the pork; season with salt and pepper. Flip the pork over and sprinkle with the remaining rosemary; season again with salt and pepper.

Set the pork in a roasting pan and roast until an instant-read thermometer inserted into the center registers 155°F, about 1½ hours. Transfer the pork to a cutting board and allow to rest for 10 minutes. Put the roasting pan on two burners over medium heat. Add the reserved wine from the cherries, stirring with a wooden spoon to scrape up all the delicious brown bits at the bottom of the pan. Stir in the stock and season with salt and pepper if necessary. Pour the pan sauce into a gravy boat.

To serve, cut off the twine and carve the pork into ½-inch-thick slices. Arrange on a serving platter with the pan sauce on the side.

HARVEY CEDARS FISH STEW
with parsley croutons

SERVES 6 TO 8 ● Every summer my family vacations in Harvey Cedars on Long Beach Island, New Jersey. Say what you want about New Jersey but let me tell you, when it comes to produce and seafood, it's hard to beat. Most people you talk to know all about the tomatoes and corn, but there is so much more. How about the clams? My family gets ours from a local clammer. The scallop boats come in daily. The swordfish is exceptional and the crabs are as good as they are anywhere. I'm inspired by all of these things, and I've included most of them in this one dish. It may seem like a lot of ingredients, and it is. If you want to leave something out go ahead, or add something to it by all means. All the action happens in one pot, making this a great beach house dish.

¾ cup extra-virgin olive oil

2 fennel bulbs (about 1½ pounds), tops removed, halved, cored, and cut into ½-inch wedges

12 garlic cloves, thinly sliced

1 large white onion, thinly sliced

1 pound littleneck clams

1 cup Pernod

1 cup dry white wine, such as Sauvignon Blanc

8 large ripe tomatoes (about 6 pounds), coarsely chopped

One 10-ounce loaf sourdough bread, sliced ½ inch thick

½ cup Parsley Sauce (page 239)

One 8-ounce bottle clam juice

2 tablespoons kosher salt

1 teaspoon freshly ground black pepper

Three 1-pound live Maine lobsters

½ pound mussels

1 pound large shrimp (about 20), peeled and deveined

1 pound jumbo sea scallops (about 10)

1 pound swordfish, cut into 1- to 1½-inch cubes

1 cup coarsely chopped fresh tarragon

1 cup fresh flat-leaf parsley, coarsely chopped

1 pound calamari, cleaned, tentacles and tubes sliced ½ inch thick

Saffron Aïoli (recipe follows; optional)

(recipe continues)

Put a 16-quart stockpot over medium-high heat and coat with the oil. When the oil starts shimmering, add the fennel, spreading it evenly in a single layer over the bottom of the pot. Brown the fennel for about 2 minutes, rotating the pieces with tongs. Add the garlic and onion and cook, stirring, until soft and fragrant, 2 to 3 minutes. Toss in the clams and give them a stir to coat with the vegetables. Pour in the Pernod, wine, and tomatoes. Cover and cook until the clams open, about 5 minutes. Using a slotted spoon or spider strainer, transfer the clams to a bowl (discard any that don't open) and set aside. Bring the liquid to a boil, turn down the heat, and simmer, stirring occasionally, until the tomatoes cook down, 15 to 20 minutes.

While the tomatoes reduce, preheat the oven to 375°F.

Spread the bread liberally with the parsley sauce. Lay the slices side by side on a baking pan. Bake for about 10 minutes, or until the bread just starts to toast.

Meanwhile, pour 2 cups water and the clam juice into the pot; season with the salt and pepper. Bring to a rapid boil over medium-high heat. Carefully ease the lobsters into the boiling liquid, cover the pot, and steam for 8 minutes, flipping them over with tongs halfway through cooking; the shells should be bright red. Using tongs, carefully remove the lobsters from the pot and put them on a large platter.

Now add the mussels, shrimp, scallops, and swordfish to the pot. Toss in the tarragon and parsley, cover, and simmer for 4 minutes.

With two large chef's knives, split the lobsters in half down the body. Place the knuckles and claws on the work surface and give them a whack to crack them open. Put the calamari and reserved clams in the pot and set the lobsters on top. Cover the pot for a minute so everything gets nice and hot; do not stir because you'll break up the fish.

For drama, I like to take the whole pot to the table and serve it in front of guests. Divide among large pasta bowls, being sure to ladle plenty of broth into each. Put a large dollop of aïoli, if using, on each crouton. Float the croutons on top of the stew. Serve the remaining croutons on the side . . . people always want another.

SAFFRON AÏOLI ● MAKES 1 CUP

Pinch of saffron threads
1 cup Best Mayonnaise (page 246) or
   quality store-bought mayo

1 tablespoon freshly squeezed lemon
   juice
4 garlic cloves, minced

Combine the saffron with 2 tablespoons warm water in a small bowl, stir, and let steep for 5 minutes to release the saffron color and flavor.

In a small bowl, whisk the mayonnaise, lemon juice, and garlic. Gradually whisk in the saffron water until well blended. Cover and store in the refrigerator for up to 5 days.

SIDES

Side dishes are one of the most important parts of dinner and they shouldn't be overlooked—or over-cooked. While I love pure, clean flavors, there's no passion or adventure in plain steamed broccoli and a baked potato. Perhaps that's why some people, especially kids, say they don't like vegetables. The sides coming up bring a ton of personality to anything you got cooking for dinner.

Vegetables are the barometers of the season. It's always exciting to see the endless variety of produce cultivated today, especially at local farm stands and CSAs (Community Supported Agriculture). With variety sprouts freedom and a bigger sandbox to play in. Don't obsess about finding exactly the same ingredients that I use here in Miami; the beauty of local produce is that it's specific to your region. Improvise and take advantage of what's best in your area, choosing the liveliest ingredients available.

SWISS CHARD AND CARAMELIZED ONION PANADE

SERVES 6 ● Panade sounds kind of "chefy" but in truth, the dish, made from crusty bread and lots of cheese, is just a cross between a savory bread pudding and holiday stuffing. When mixed with eggs and cream, the bread softens so it becomes almost soufflé-like, with pillows of puffy goodness infused with chard and caramelized onions. If something can be peasant food and elegant at once, this is it! Pair this as a side with Whole Roasted Chicken with Plumped Raisins, Toasted Pine Nuts, and Arugula (page 142) or serve it with a simple green salad, and you've got dinner.

1 bunch Swiss chard (about ¾ pound)

2 tablespoons extra-virgin olive oil

1 large white onion, thinly sliced

Kosher salt and freshly ground black pepper

2 garlic cloves, smashed and chopped

1 crusty sourdough baguette, cut into 1-inch pieces (6 cups)

1 tablespoon unsalted butter, for the dish

2 cups chicken stock

½ cup heavy cream

3 large egg yolks

6 ounces Fontina cheese, shredded (about 2 cups)

1 cup freshly grated Parmesan cheese

Cut the ribs out of the Swiss chard and set aside. Roll the leaves into a bundle and coarsely chop into 1-inch ribbons. Put the chopped leaves in a colander and rinse well. Set aside to drain. Cut the ribs crosswise into ¼-inch pieces.

Put a large pot over high heat and coat with the oil. Add the onion and season with salt and pepper. Cook, stirring with a wooden spoon, until the onion is golden brown and caramelized, about 8 minutes. Add the chard ribs and continue to cook until soft, about 4 minutes. Add the garlic, give it a stir, and cook for a minute until fragrant. Toss in the chard leaves. Turn the leaves over until the chard wilts, releases its moisture, and cooks down, roughly

(recipe continues)

3 minutes. Season again with salt and pepper. Put the bread cubes in a large bowl and dump the Swiss chard mixture on top.

Preheat the oven to 325°F. Butter an 8 × 8-inch baking dish. Also butter the dull side of a piece of foil large enough to cover the dish.

Return the pot (no need to clean it) to medium heat and pour in the stock and cream. While they are heating, whisk the egg yolks in a stainless steel bowl until they increase slightly in volume. Gradually whisk the hot stock mixture into the yolks (do not add it too quickly or the eggs will scramble). Pour the mixture over the bread and chard. Add the Fontina, season with salt and pepper, and toss to combine.

Pour the bread mixture into the buttered dish and spread evenly. Sprinkle the Parmesan evenly on top. Cover the baking dish tightly with the foil, buttered side down.

Fill a roasting pan with ½ inch of water. Carefully place the baking dish in the water bath and put in the oven. Bake until the center jiggles slightly when you shake the dish, about 1 hour. Remove the panade from the oven and water bath and remove the foil. Switch the oven to broil.

Stick the panade under the broiler for 3 minutes to brown the cheese. To serve, scoop the panade out with a spoon.

BRAISED COLLARD GREENS
with bacon and soy sauce

SERVES 6 ● Collard greens with bacon or ham are a classic—spicy, smoky, and tender in an addictive savory broth. Most recipes splash in some vinegar to add a little tang and balance the bitterness of the greens. Soy sauce adds a different spin to this Southern staple. Try this alongside Thyme-Smoked Four-Inch Porterhouse Steak (page 168) or Whole Roasted Chicken with Plumped Raisins, Toasted Pine Nuts, and Arugula (page 142).

3 pounds young collard greens (about 6 bunches)

¼ pound (6 slices) Maple-Cured Bacon (page 230) or store-bought thick-cut bacon, cut into ½-inch pieces

1 onion, thinly sliced

2 garlic cloves, minced

2 cups chicken stock

Kosher salt and freshly ground black pepper

¼ cup soy sauce

2 tablespoons unsalted butter

Cut the tough stalks and stems from the collards and discard any leaves that are bruised or yellow. Collard greens tend to have a bit of dirt and sand trapped between the leaves, so you need to wash them a few times. Fill the sink with water and wash the collards thoroughly, swishing the leaves around to remove the dirt. Drain and repeat until the water runs clear. Dry the greens thoroughly. Stack up several leaves, roll them into a cigar, and cut them into 1-inch ribbons. Repeat until all the leaves are shredded.

Put a large pot over medium heat. When the pot is hot, add the bacon and fry until it gets crisp and renders its fat, about 4 minutes. Remove with a slotted spoon and set aside on a paper towel–lined plate. Add the onion and garlic to the fat and cook, stirring, until they begin to soften and get a little color, about 5 minutes. Pack in the greens, pushing them down into the pot and turning them over with a wooden spoon so the leaves hit the heat and begin to wilt. Pour in the stock and season with salt and pepper. Give everything a good stir and cover the pot. Reduce the heat to low and simmer the collards for 1 hour.

Stir in the soy sauce, and taste the "pot liquor" (broth) for seasoning, adding more salt and pepper to your taste. Stir in the butter until melted. Transfer the collard greens to a serving bowl and scatter the bacon on top.

ROASTED CAULIFLOWER
with parsley sauce

SERVES 6 ● Cauliflower can be a little bland on its own, but blasting the florets in a hot oven concentrates their natural sweetness and transforms the lily-white vegetable to a crisp caramel-brown. Tossing the roasted cauliflower with emerald green parsley sauce brightens the charred flavor. This is a universal side that goes with everything.

1 head cauliflower (2 to 3 pounds), cut into florets
¼ cup extra-virgin olive oil

2 teaspoons kosher salt
1 teaspoon freshly ground black pepper
½ cup Parsley Sauce (page 239)

Preheat the oven to 450°F.

Put the cauliflower in a mixing bowl and toss with the oil, salt, and pepper. Spread the cauliflower out on a baking sheet. Roast, shaking the pan halfway through cooking, until tender and slightly charred, 40 to 45 minutes. Return the cauliflower to the bowl and toss with the parsley sauce to coat evenly. Serve hot.

ROASTED BUTTERNUT SQUASH with sage, maple syrup, and pecorino

SERVES 4 ● With just a handful of ingredients, this fall favorite is super easy to make and at the same time really comforting. The mild sweetness of butternut squash mingling with the rich nuttiness of brown butter and the delicate, woodsy aroma of sage is downright delicious. Cutting up butternut squash is a notoriously difficult task because of its thickness and density. The most important thing to remember when cutting winter squash is to keep the piece you are working on as stable as possible.

One 1½-pound butternut squash

2 tablespoons extra-virgin olive oil

1 teaspoon kosher salt

½ teaspoon freshly ground black pepper

2 tablespoons unsalted butter

5 fresh sage leaves

2 tablespoons maple syrup

¼ cup freshly grated Pecorino cheese

Preheat the oven to 450°F.

Using a serrated knife, cut off about ¼ inch from the bottom of the squash and also from the stem end. Cut the squash crosswise in half to separate the neck from the bulb. Stand the squash halves upright on a cutting board, cut side down, and cut off the skin with the knife, turning the squash as you go. Now, cut the 2 pieces of peeled squash from top to bottom down the middle so you have 4 pieces. Scoop out the seeds and strings from the bulb. Slice the squash in ½-inch-thick half moons.

Put the squash in a bowl and add the oil, salt, and pepper; toss to coat. Arrange the slices side by side on a baking sheet; it is okay if they overlap a little. Roast for 20 minutes, or until the squash has a golden color and is tender when pierced with a fork. Transfer the squash to a serving platter.

Melt the butter in a small skillet over medium heat. Then cook it, swirling the pan around, until the milk solids sink to the bottom of the pan and the butter becomes a nut-brown color and has a toasty aroma. Add the sage and let it fry and pop for 2 or 3 seconds, then immediately stir in the maple syrup. Remove the pan from the heat and drizzle the brown butter over the squash right away. Sprinkle the Pecorino all over the top.

CHEESE GRITS

SERVES 6 ● Grits get a bad rap, man. Most of the time grits are watery and served with greasy eggs in a diner. Grits can be so much more! By using good-quality coarsely ground grits and cooking them right, you can easily elevate this Southern staple. Serve with Slow-Roasted Pork Shoulder with Pickled Onions (page 162).

2 cups white coarse-ground grits,
  preferably Anson Mills
Kosher salt
4 tablespoons (½ stick) unsalted butter

½ cup whole milk
¼ pound sharp white Cheddar cheese,
  shredded (1 cup)
½ teaspoon freshly ground black pepper

Put the grits in a heavy-bottomed pot, cover with 5 cups water, and set over medium heat. Bring to a simmer, then reduce the heat to low. Stir constantly with a wooden spoon until the grits begin to thicken, 5 to 8 minutes. Cover the pot and continue to cook over low heat, stirring every 10 minutes or so, and adding a little hot water if the grits become too thick. If a spoon can stand upright, then the grits are too thick.

After 30 minutes, add 1 tablespoon salt. Continue to cook the grits, covered, until they are creamy and tender but not mushy, about 30 minutes more.

Uncover the pot and stir in the butter, milk, cheese, and pepper. Add more salt, if needed.

BRAISED FENNEL with pernod and tarragon

SERVES 6 ● For all the licorice lovers out there, this one's for you. Raw fennel can be a bit much for some people, but braising fennel mellows out its strong anise taste, making it a bit sweeter and meltingly tender. Pernod and tarragon amp up the anise flavor, rounding out this all-purpose, easy-as-can-be side. It's especially good with steamed white fish and pork chops.

2 tablespoons extra-virgin olive oil

3 fennel bulbs (about 2 pounds), tops removed, quartered or cut into wedges depending on size, core intact

¼ cup Pernod

¼ cup dry white wine, such as Sauvignon Blanc

Kosher salt and freshly ground black pepper

1 cup chicken stock

1 tablespoon unsalted butter

1 tablespoon chopped fresh tarragon

Put a Dutch oven or large pot over medium-high heat and coat with the oil. When the oil is hot, lay the fennel in the pot. Brown it well, turning once, about 8 minutes total.

Pour in the Pernod and wine and cook until the liquid evaporates, a minute or two. Season with salt and pepper and pour in the stock. Cover and reduce the heat to medium-low. Braise the fennel, turning halfway through cooking, until tender, 20 minutes. You want the liquid to be just about cooked down by the time the fennel is tender.

Remove the fennel from the heat and stir in the butter. Arrange the fennel on a platter and garnish with the tarragon.

SAUTÉED BROCCOLI RABE
with farro, crushed red pepper, and lemon

SERVES 4 ● Broccoli rabe is one of those vegetables that people either love or hate. An acquired taste, the subtle pungent bitterness of this healthy green fits with any main course. Farro's nuttiness rounds out this simple and rustic side. It also makes a fine vegetarian dinner.

½ cup farro

2 pounds broccoli rabe, ends trimmed, cut into 1-inch pieces

2 tablespoons extra-virgin olive oil

2 garlic cloves, minced

¼ teaspoon crushed red pepper flakes

Kosher salt and freshly ground black pepper

Zest of 1 lemon

Bring a medium pot of salted water to a boil. Add the farro, reduce the heat to medium-low, and cover. Simmer until the farro is tender and the grains have split open, about 30 minutes. Remove the farro from the pot with a spider strainer or mesh sieve, put it in a colander, and rinse with cool water. Set aside. Keep the cooking water in the pot.

Bring the cooking liquid back up to a boil and season again with salt. The farro will have soaked up much of the original seasoning. Boil the broccoli rabe until just tender, about 3 minutes. It should still be firm as it will finish cooking in the skillet. Drain in a colander.

Set a large skillet over medium heat and coat with the oil. When the oil is hot, add the garlic and cook, stirring, for a minute to soften. Add the broccoli rabe and red pepper; season with 1 teaspoon salt and ½ teaspoon black pepper. Toss the rabe to coat with the oil and cook until tender, roughly 5 minutes. Add the drained farro, tossing to combine, and sauté for another minute until heated through.

To serve, put the broccoli rabe and farro on a nice platter. Finely grate lemon zest over the top, preferably with a Microplane. (I find if you grate the zest ahead of time, it gets clumpy and doesn't distribute evenly.)

ROASTED GARLIC MASHED POTATOES

SERVES 4 ● I've never met anyone who doesn't like mashed potatoes, an all-American dish that is nostalgic and satisfying. Yukon Gold potatoes have a buttery aroma and a rich, creamy flavor, while roasted garlic adds a sweet flavor that is less aggressive than that of raw garlic. These are great with Pan-Roasted Half Boneless Chicken with Sautéed Escarole (page 140).

4 medium Yukon Gold potatoes (1½ pounds), peeled and quartered

Kosher salt

1 cup whole milk, or more as needed

4 tablespoons (½ stick) unsalted butter, cut into chunks

¼ cup Roasted Garlic Puree (page 238)

½ teaspoon freshly ground black pepper

Put the potatoes in a large pot, cover with cold water, and add 1 tablespoon salt. Bring to a boil over medium heat, then reduce the heat so the water simmers gently. Cook until there is no resistance when a fork is inserted into the potatoes, about 20 minutes.

Warm the milk in a small pot over low heat.

Drain the potatoes and, while they're hot, pass them through a food mill or potato ricer into a large mixing bowl. (If you do not have a ricer or food mill you can use a potato masher, but the potatoes won't be as fluffy.) Add the milk, butter, and garlic puree, stirring with a wooden spoon to blend into the potatoes; season with 1 teaspoon salt and the pepper. Feel free to add more milk to achieve the consistency that you like. Cover and keep the potatoes warm until ready to serve.

DESSERTS

Michael's Genuine pastry chef Hedy Goldsmith makes the best desserts of anyone I know . . . and I know a lot of people. She has this gift for creating dishes that have an inner logic and make sense without being obnoxious or obvious. Everything is fully balanced on the palate: not too sweet, with a faint hint of salt, a bit of acid, some crunch, and a creamy finish. Truth be told, I'm not big into baking. My goal here is to take Hedy's lead and feature down-to-earth desserts that riff on familiar, timeless flavors, like doughnuts made from store-bought biscuit dough and classic lemon pudding cake that tastes even better than you remember as a kid.

The reality is very few people have the time or desire to make dessert every day. Most often, people get motivated to bake when sharing a meal with loved ones or cooking for a special occasion. Some of these recipes are super simple while others are slightly more involved, but all are totally doable. You don't have to be a pastry chef to master them, you just need a sweet tooth!

QUICK DOUGHNUTS with anise sugar and orange marmalade

MAKES 16 DOUGHNUTS ● If you have ever tried to make homemade doughnuts, you know that the process can be a bit of a hassle. But transforming store-bought biscuit dough into delicious golden doughnuts could not be easier, seriously. The slightly crunchy texture of fried dough dusted with anise sugar is a perfect complement to tangy orange marmalade.

Canola oil, for frying

1 cup sugar

1 tablespoon anise seed

Two 16.3-ounce tubes Pillsbury Grands! refrigerated buttermilk biscuit dough

1 cup orange marmalade

Heat 3 inches of oil to 325°F in a countertop electric fryer or deep pot. If you don't have a deep-fry thermometer, a good way to test if the oil is hot enough is to stick the end of a wooden spoon or chopstick in it. If bubbles circle around the end, then you're good to go.

In a medium bowl, combine the sugar and anise seed.

Open the tubes of biscuits and pull the individual pieces apart to give you 16 doughnuts. Fry a couple of pieces at a time, keeping an eye on maintaining the oil temperature. As the doughnuts puff up and rise to the surface, flip them over with a slotted spoon, skimmer, or chopsticks. They should take roughly 2 minutes on each side. Carefully remove the doughnuts from the oil and transfer directly into the bowl of anise sugar, tossing to coat evenly.

Fit a small pastry bag with a large tip and fill with the orange marmalade. Poke a hole into the middle of each doughnut with the tip and pipe the marmalade inside the doughnuts to fill. These are best served warm.

MILK CHOCOLATE CREMOSO
with espresso parfait

SERVES 6 ● This decadent milk chocolate cremoso—a silky puddinglike dessert—is drizzled with olive oil for an unexpected pop of flavor. Some people are like, whoa . . . olive oil and chocolate? But the combo really works. The hazelnuts and chocolate bring forward a Nutella-like flavor, and the salt cuts the sweetness. The slight sourness of crisp sourdough bread and smoky flavor of espresso deepen the complexity of the dish. A recipe is only as good as its ingredients, and this is no exception. Use the best-quality chocolate—it makes all the difference between a waxy, vaguely chocolaty flavor and intense chocolatiness. Valrhona, Lindt, and Scharffen Berger are premium chocolates I like. Most of this dessert can be made ahead, so it's perfect to serve for a dinner party.

CREMOSO
10 ounces milk chocolate, finely chopped
   (1½ cups)
1⅓ cups heavy cream
3 tablespoons granulated sugar
3 large egg yolks

ESPRESSO PARFAIT
1⅓ cups heavy cream
⅓ cup confectioners' sugar
1 teaspoon pure vanilla extract
1½ tablespoons brewed espresso, cooled

GARNISH
⅓ cup chopped hazelnuts, toasted (see
   Note, page 54)
Extra-virgin olive oil
Coarse sea salt
6 thin slices sourdough bread, toasted

To make the cremoso, put the chocolate in a heatproof bowl. Combine the cream and sugar in a pot over medium heat and bring to a boil. In a large bowl, whisk the egg yolks until slightly thick and yellow. Whisking constantly, slowly add the hot cream to the egg yolks. Do not add it too quickly or the eggs will scramble. Return the eggs to the pot and whisk over medium-low heat until the custard is thick enough to coat the back of a spoon, about 2 minutes; do not boil.

(recipe continues)

Pour the hot cream mixture over the chocolate and whisk thoroughly until the chocolate is melted and smooth. Cover and chill the cremoso until completely firm, at least 6 hours or, even better, overnight. The cremoso can easily be prepared a day or two in advance.

To make the parfait, whip the cream with the confectioners' sugar and vanilla to soft peaks. Gently fold in the espresso and spoon into 6 small (3- to 4-ounce) ramekins. Cover with plastic wrap and freeze for at least 1 hour or up to overnight.

To serve, set aside about 2 teaspoons hazelnuts for garnish; divide the remainder among 6 dessert plates. Dip a metal tablespoon into hot water for a couple of seconds to heat up. Wipe the spoon dry with a kitchen towel and run the spoon along the cremoso to make a long wave that barrels over itself. Spoon the cremoso on top of the hazelnuts. Drizzle with olive oil and sprinkle with sea salt. Top each serving with a slice of sourdough toast, and set a ramekin of the parfait on the side. Sprinkle with the reserved nuts.

BANANA TOFFEE PANINI

SERVES 4 ● I totally owe this one to the brilliant simplicity of Hedy Goldsmith. A dessert panini? Why didn't I think of that?! Now, dessert panini might not be your first thought, but this recipe brings a sweet new definition to the sandwich, tasting like a warm banana split in a cocoon of rich bread. If you own a panini press, then you already know that it invariably turns a regular sandwich into something irresistible. The texture contrast between the crunchy exterior and the soft, gooey interior is a big part of the sex appeal. The fleur de sel makes this dish; without the salty balance it would be way too sweet. This panini also rocks for brunch.

3 tablespoons granulated sugar

1 teaspoon ground cinnamon

4 tablespoons (½ stick) unsalted butter, at room temperature

Eight ¾-inch slices brioche or challah

2 tablespoons dulce de leche or caramel sauce

4 very ripe bananas, halved lengthwise and crosswise

½ cup crushed toffee pieces, such as Heath

4 pinches of fleur de sel or other coarse sea salt

2 tablespoons sweetened condensed milk

Confectioners' sugar, for dusting

1 cup Chocolate Sauce (recipe follows)

Preheat a sandwich press according to the manufacturer's instructions. If you don't have an electric press, place a grill pan or heavy skillet over medium-high heat.

When building the sandwiches, make sure to distribute the ingredients evenly across the bread so the sandwiches press flat. First, combine the sugar and cinnamon in a small bowl. Spread butter on one side of each slice of bread and sprinkle with the cinnamon sugar. Flip the bread over and spread with dulce de leche on the other side.

Arrange 4 slices of banana on top of the dulce de leche on 4 of the slices of bread, then sprinkle with toffee pieces and salt. Drizzle sweetened condensed milk on top. Cover each with the remaining 4 slices of bread, dulce de leche side down, to make 4 sandwiches.

(recipe continues)

Put the sandwiches in the panini maker or grill pan. Close the press (or, if using a pan, place another heavy pan on top of the sandwich to press it down). Grill until the brioche is crisp on both sides and the cinnamon sugar caramelizes, about 2 minutes. (If you're cooking the sandwich in a pan on the stove, after 3 minutes flip it over with a spatula to crisp the other side for a couple of minutes.)

Transfer the panini to a cutting board and cut into quarters. Dust with confectioners' sugar and serve with chocolate sauce on the side for dipping.

CHOCOLATE SAUCE ● MAKES ABOUT 2 CUPS

1 cup heavy cream
1 tablespoon unsalted butter

½ pound semisweet chocolate, chopped into chunks (about 1¾ cups)

Heat the cream and butter in a pot over medium heat. Once steam rises from the surface, add the chocolate, and stir until it's melted and smooth. Remove from the heat and let cool to room temperature. You can store the sauce in a covered container in the fridge for up to 10 days. Rewarm before serving.

MANGO UPSIDE-DOWN CAKE
with basil ice cream

SERVES 8 TO 10 ● Fresh fruit caramelized and embedded in rich buttery cake makes a great dessert any time of year. Just about any seasonal fruit that you have on hand works very well in this recipe. Try peaches, apricots, and, of course, pineapple. The beauty of this one-pan cake is its simplicity: you don't even need a cake pan.

If the basil in your herb garden has, like mine, grown to the size of a bush, and you've had your fill of pesto, consider trying the basil ice cream recipe. Basil is a super fruity and floral herb, which to me is a natural for ice cream. When people take their first bite, the reaction is always the same: oh my God!

4 tablespoons (½ stick) unsalted butter

¾ cup packed light brown sugar

Two 1-pound firm-ripe mangoes, peeled, pitted, and cut into ½-inch slices

1½ cups all-purpose flour

3 tablespoons cornmeal

1 teaspoon baking powder

¼ teaspoon fine salt

8 tablespoons (1 stick) unsalted butter, softened

1 cup plus 1 tablespoon granulated sugar

1 teaspoon pure vanilla extract

4 large eggs, separated

⅔ cup buttermilk

Basil Ice Cream (recipe follows), optional

Put a 10-inch cast-iron skillet over medium heat and add the 4 tablespoons butter. When the butter is melted, stir in the brown sugar. Simmer, stirring occasionally, until the mixture looks like caramel, about 5 minutes. Swirl the pan around so the caramel covers the bottom completely. Remove from the heat. Tightly fan the mango slices over the caramel in concentric circles to cover the entire bottom, overlapping the slices.

Preheat the oven to 350°F.

In a mixing bowl, whisk together the flour, cornmeal, baking powder, and salt. In another bowl, beat the softened butter with a handheld electric mixer on medium-high speed. Gradually sprinkle in 1 cup sugar and continue beating until light and fluffy, about 5 minutes. Beat in the vanilla and egg

(recipe continues)

yolks, one at a time, scraping the sides of the bowl with a rubber spatula if necessary.

Reduce the mixer speed to low and add half of the dry ingredients, mixing until just combined. Stir in the buttermilk, then add the remaining dry ingredients, stirring to incorporate.

Beat the egg whites in another bowl with cleaned beaters until frothy. Sprinkle in the remaining 1 tablespoon sugar and continue to beat until the whites hold stiff peaks. Gently fold half of the beaten whites into the batter with a rubber spatula to lighten it. Then fold in the remaining whites; it's okay if some white streaks remain.

Pour the batter over the mangoes and spread evenly to the edges of the skillet. Bake until the cake is golden brown and a toothpick comes out clean when inserted into the center, 45 to 50 minutes.

Cool the cake in the pan for 5 minutes. Run a knife around the inside rim of the pan to loosen it from the sides and make sure the cake will come out easily. Set a serving plate firmly on top of the pan and carefully flip it over to invert the cake onto the plate. Cool before serving with basil ice cream, if desired.

(recipe continues)

BASIL ICE CREAM ● MAKES 1 QUART

2 cups packed fresh basil leaves

½ cup sugar

2 cups heavy cream

1 cup whole milk

1 vanilla bean, halved lengthwise

8 large egg yolks

Pinch of salt

In a food processor, combine the basil and sugar. Pulse until very finely ground. The sugar should be bright green and look almost like pesto.

Combine the cream, milk, and basil-sugar in a large pot over medium heat. Scrape out the seeds of the vanilla bean and add them to the cream mixture; put the pod in there too for extra flavor. Simmer gently, stirring, until the sugar is dissolved, about 5 minutes. Ideally, the temperature should reach 175°F (just scalding); this should take 5 to 8 minutes.

In a large mixing bowl, whisk the egg yolks until slightly thick and yellow. Gradually whisk half of the hot cream into the yolk mixture (do not add it too quickly or the eggs will scramble). Return the entire mixture to the pot and whisk constantly over medium-low heat until the custard is thick enough to coat the back of a spoon and leaves a path when you run your finger across it, about 5 minutes; do not allow to boil.

Pass the custard through a fine-mesh sieve into a large container. Chill the ice cream base completely in a large bowl full of ice water, stirring here and there. Mix in the salt once completely cold.

Churn in an ice cream maker according to the manufacturer's directions. When done, the ice cream will be the consistency of soft serve. To harden the ice cream fully, freeze in a covered plastic container.

MEYER LEMON PUDDING CAKE with chantilly cream and fresh blueberries

SERVES 6 ● Like magic, this lemon pudding cake separates into two layers during baking: an airy and soufflé-like cake on top, and a soft lemony curd below. In truth, the first time I ate it I was convinced it was a cake and pudding recipe combined. This foolproof recipe is the perfect summer sweet, served simply with fresh berries and whipped cream. For the creamiest texture, it is important to bake the cake in a water bath. The hot water protects the cake from cooking too quickly, keeping the pudding super supple.

Unsalted butter, for the baking dish
2 Meyer lemons
¼ cup all-purpose flour
½ teaspoon kosher salt
¾ cup sugar

3 large eggs, separated
1½ cups whole milk
Chantilly Cream (recipe follows)
Fresh blueberries

INGREDIENT NOTE

meyer lemon

Meyer lemons have a bright, balanced lemon flavor with moderate acidity, and are a bit sweeter than their everyday counterparts. When they are in season in the fall and winter, I take full advantage of them. If Meyer lemons are not available, substitute regular lemons mixed with a couple tablespoons of orange juice.

Preheat the oven to 350°F. Lightly butter a 1½-quart soufflé, gratin, or other ceramic baking dish, or 6 (6-ounce) individual baking dishes. Set inside a 9 × 13-inch baking dish or even a roasting pan. Bring a kettle of water to a boil for the water bath.

Finely grate the zest from the lemons, and then squeeze out the juice; you should have roughly 1 tablespoon zest and ⅓ cup juice.

Whisk together the flour, salt, and ½ cup of the sugar in a mixing bowl.

(recipe continues)

In another bowl, beat the egg whites with an electric mixer until they hold soft peaks. Beat in the remaining ¼ cup sugar, a little at a time, and continue to beat until the whites hold stiff, glossy peaks. In a separate large bowl, whisk together the yolks, milk, zest, and juice. Add the flour mixture, whisking until just combined. Gently fold half of the beaten whites into the batter with a rubber spatula to lighten it. Then fold in the remaining whites, taking care not to deflate them; it's okay if some white streaks remain. The batter will be on the thin side and won't look like regular cake batter.

Pour the batter into the soufflé dish (or individual dishes). Put the larger pan in the oven, with the soufflé dish inside it, and fill the larger pan with boiling water to come about halfway up the sides. It's best to do this right on the oven rack so you don't move the pans again and risk splashing water into the batter. Bake until the cake is puffed and golden, 40 to 45 minutes. Serve the cake hot from the oven or let it cool a bit until warm. Spoon the pudding cake into small dessert bowls, being sure to get some of the lemon pudding at the bottom of the dish. Top with chantilly cream and blueberries.

CHANTILLY CREAM ● MAKES ABOUT 1 CUP

½ cup heavy cream, cold

1 tablespoon confectioners' sugar

Chill a mixing bowl and wire whisk in the freezer for 10 minutes before beginning. Whisk the cream in the chilled bowl until it begins to foam and thicken up. Add the sugar and continue to beat until the cream just holds soft peaks. Do not overwhip. Feel free to use an immersion blender with the whisk attachment or a handheld electric mixer if you don't want to whip by hand.

TOASTED-ALMOND PANNA COTTA with maple roasted pears

SERVES 6 ● In the scheme of desserts, panna cotta is not only one of the lightest, it's thankfully also one of the easiest and fastest to prepare. The eggless custard sets with gelatin, but what really matters is the quantity used. If you have a heavy hand, then the result is more like cement Jell-O than melt-in-your-mouth. The infusion of the almonds adds a nutty-creamy flavor that's satisfying without being cloying. Roasted pears set the whole thing off with a balance of texture and fruitiness.

2 cups whole raw almonds

2 cups heavy cream

½ cup sugar

1 vanilla bean, halved lengthwise

Pinch of kosher salt

4 gelatin sheets or one ¼-ounce envelope
  powdered unflavored gelatin
  (2 teaspoons)

2½ cups buttermilk

Maple Roasted Pears (recipe follows)

Candied almonds

Preheat the oven to 300°F.

Put the almonds in a food processor and pulse a few times until they are coarsely chopped. Spread the almonds on a baking sheet. Bake until lightly toasted and fragrant, about 10 minutes.

Combine the cream and sugar in a pot over medium heat. Scrape out the seeds of the vanilla bean and add to the cream mixture; put the pod in there too for extra flavor. Simmer, stirring to dissolve the sugar, until steam rises from the top of the pot. Remove from the heat and stir in the nuts and salt. Cover and let the nuts steep in the cream for 30 minutes.

Soak the gelatin sheets in cold water for 3 minutes to soften, then remove and squeeze out the excess water (if using powdered gelatin, no need to strain out the water).

Pass the almond mixture through a fine-mesh sieve, pressing on the solids with the back of a wooden spoon to extract all of the almond flavor. Discard the solids. Add the softened gelatin while the mixture is still warm, stirring to incorporate. Stir in the buttermilk.

Carefully fill 6 straight-sided rocks glasses halfway with the custard; pour carefully so you don't get schmutz on the sides of the glasses. Cover loosely and chill in the refrigerator until firm, at least 8 hours or, even better, overnight.

To serve, set a couple of roasted pear wedges on top of each chilled panna cotta. Garnish with candied almonds.

MAPLE ROASTED PEARS

Nonstick spray	¼ cup packed dark brown sugar
3 ripe but firm pears, such as Comice	¼ cup maple syrup
or red or green Bartletts	3 tablespoons brandy or bourbon
¼ cup molasses	½ teaspoon pure vanilla extract

Preheat the oven to 400°F. Coat a rimmed baking sheet with nonstick spray.

Using a vegetable peeler, peel the skin from the pears. Slice each pear into 6 wedges and carefully cut out the core with a paring knife.

In a mixing bowl, combine the molasses, sugar, syrup, brandy, and vanilla. Add the pear wedges, tossing to coat. Dump the pears onto the baking sheet in a single layer. Roast for 20 minutes total, turning the pears with tongs halfway through cooking, until they are soft and brown. Remove from the oven and cool until warm. Save the caramel left on the baking sheet; it's terrific drizzled on ice cream.

DRINKS

Wine is great but sometimes you want to flex your muscles, get the evening hopping, and make it a night to remember. My only requirements when it comes to cocktails are that they don't require a thousand ingredients, are natural—without any artificial anything—and are totally delicious. When I'm entertaining at home, I strive to keep it simple; I don't want to be stuck playing bartender all night.

I'm not a huge fan of vodka or gin, so the cocktails that follow showcase different spirits, like St. Germain elderflower liqueur and Campari. I can't deal with drinks that try too hard, are in-your-face abrasive, and sugary sweet. These are really smooth, well balanced, and understated. There are also a couple of virgin sodas that add pizzazz to any picnic.

PASSION FRUIT SODA

SERVES 2 ● This combo was born out of the remake of a classic cocktail, the Hurricane. Passion fruit adds a tropical flavor and I just love the crunch of the seeds. The result is a tantalizing and refreshing mix using one of South Florida's most delicious fruits.

2 ounces (¼ cup) fresh passion fruit pulp and seeds

2 ounces (¼ cup) freshly squeezed orange juice

2 ounces (¼ cup) freshly squeezed lime juice

2 ounces (¼ cup) agave nectar

Ginger ale

Fresh mint leaves, for garnish

Stir together the passion fruit, orange juice, lime juice, and agave in a measuring cup.

Fill 2 highball glasses with ice and divide the fruit mixture between them. Top each off with ginger ale. Garnish with mint sprigs.

ORANGE GINA SODA

SERVES 2 ● This effervescent soda is a homemade variation of the popular soft drink. Fresh and bright, it's the perfect post-yoga refresher. Put a little pizzazz in your day and try this wonderful fruity elixir.

4 ounces (½ cup) freshly squeezed orange juice

2 ounces (¼ cup) agave nectar

Juice of 1 lime

Seltzer

2 orange slices

Stir together the orange juice, agave, and lime juice in a measuring cup. Fill 2 highball glasses with ice and divide the OJ mixture between them. Top each off with seltzer. Garnish with a slice of orange.

THE SOMBRITA

SERVES 2 ● A take on the margarita, this drink has Sombra mezcal, which greets your palate with a smoky introduction. The inherent peppery notes of mezcal and jalapeño are cooled by fresh pineapple and cucumber and balanced by fragrant cardamom. Mezcal is fermented and distilled from agave, so a splash of the nectar ties the flavors together.

2 pineapple wedges

6 thin slices cucumber, plus more for garnish

Splash of agave nectar

1 thin slice jalapeño

2 cardamom pods

4 ounces (½ cup) Sombra mezcal

In a martini shaker or wide glass, combine the pineapple, cucumber, agave, jalapeño, and cardamom. Using a muddler or the handle of a wooden spoon, smash and crush everything together to release the juice. When you have some nice juice in there, add a handful or two of ice. Fill with the mezcal and shake to combine. Fill 2 rocks glasses with ice and strain the cocktail into the glasses. Garnish each with a slice of cucumber.

OLD-FASHIONED SIDECAR

SERVES 2 ● Call this a new Old-Fashioned. I replace the dated syrupy orange liqueur with fresh agave, which is essentially a citrus-type honey grown in the arid hillsides of Mexico.

4 ounces (½ cup) Cognac, such as
    Courvoisier VS
1 ounce (2 tablespoons) agave nectar

1 ounce (2 tablespoons) freshly squeezed
    lemon juice
2 lemon wedges

Combine the Cognac, agave, and lemon juice in a shaker with ice; shake it up really well to break the ice into shards. Strain the cocktail into 2 chilled martini glasses and garnish each with a lemon wedge.

THE NEWGRONI

SERVES 2 ● The classic Campari-based cocktail, the Negroni, is equal parts Campari, gin, and sweet vermouth. Starting with the classic formula but then deviating from it, I replace the piney flavor of gin with the naturally acidic apple and pear, boosted by the warmth of Calvados apple brandy. The orange bitters give the drink a dry finish so it's not overly sweet.

1 Granny Smith apple, cut into wedges
1 Bosc pear, cut into wedges
1 teaspoon fresh thyme leaves
3 ounces (6 tablespoons) Campari
3 ounces (6 tablespoons) Calvados

2 ounces (¼ cup) Simple Syrup
    (page 224)
Seltzer
2 dashes of orange bitters

Put the apple, pear, and thyme through a vegetable juicer. You should get about ½ cup juice.

Divide the Campari and Calvados between 2 chilled highball glasses. Into each, pour ¼ cup of the fruit juice, 1 ounce (2 tablespoons) simple syrup, a splash of seltzer, and a dash of orange bitters. Stir to combine.

BULLETPROOF MANHATTAN

SERVES 2 ● I'm a bourbon drinker, and this reinvented classic cocktail shows off my favorite whiskey in style. I replace the typically used sweet vermouth with the deep sweet-and-sour flavor of cherries, balanced by the spicy undertone of fresh rosemary and warmth of good bourbon.

One 8-ounce jar Amarena Italian cherries
  or any quality jarred or canned cherries
  in syrup

1 fresh rosemary sprig, plus more for
  garnish
4 ounces (½ cup) bourbon
Juice of ½ lemon

Strain the cherry syrup into a small pot and add ½ cup water. Toss in the rosemary and place over medium heat. Simmer for 2 to 3 minutes, remove from the heat, and let the rosemary steep in the cherry syrup as it cools to infuse the flavor. Once cool, put the cherries back in the syrup and chill in the refrigerator for at least 1 to 2 days.

Combine the bourbon, lemon juice, and 2 ounces (¼ cup) of the cherry syrup in a shaker with ice; shake it up really well to break the ice into shards. Strain the cocktail into 2 chilled martini glasses. Spear a couple of cherries each on 2 rosemary sprigs and use to garnish the cocktail.

THE CANDIDATE

SERVES 2 ● It's the drink that propelled Obama to the White House! Well not exactly, but this cocktail will gather all parties together harmoniously around the table, just like its ingredients in the glass. Canton (a liqueur made from Chinese baby ginger) is a less abrasive alternative to fresh ginger, which can sometimes overwhelm a drink if not used properly.

4 ounces (½ cup) Scotch, such as Chivas
  Regal 12-year Scotch whiskey
1 ounce (2 tablespoons) ginger liqueur,
  such as Domaine de Canton

½ ounce (1 tablespoon) freshly squeezed
  lemon juice
½ ounce (1 tablespoon) Simple Syrup
  (recipe follows)
Crystallized ginger wheels

Combine the Scotch, ginger liqueur, lemon juice, and simple syrup in a shaker with ice; shake it up really well to break the ice into shards. Strain the cocktail into 2 chilled martini glasses and garnish each with crystallized ginger.

SIMPLE SYRUP ● MAKES ABOUT 1 CUP

1 cup sugar

1 cup water

Combine the sugar and water in a pot over medium heat. Gently simmer for 2 minutes, swirling the pot now and then, until the sugar is dissolved and the liquid becomes clear. Do not allow the syrup to boil or get dark.

Cool completely and use to sweeten mixed drinks or iced tea. Keeps nearly indefinitely, refrigerated.

CABARETE

SERVES 2 ● This drink transforms a standard Champagne cocktail into something a bit more zesty and floral. Bright orange in color, Aperol is a light aperitif with a unique bittersweet taste that blends beautifully with fruit and bubbly. Making watermelon juice is a snap; simply pop a wedge of seedless watermelon (without rind) into a blender, turn it on for two seconds, turn it off, and you're done.

3 ounces (6 tablespoons) Aperol Italian
   liqueur
3 ounces (6 tablespoons) elderflower
   liqueur, such as St. Germain
Champagne or sparkling wine

Seltzer
2 ounces (¼ cup) fresh watermelon juice
2 dashes of orange bitters
Candied watermelon rind (optional)

Divide the Aperol and elderflower liqueur between 2 chilled wine glasses filled with ice. Fill the glasses with Champagne, and after the foam subsides, pour in seltzer to reach almost to the top of the glass. Add 2 tablespoons watermelon juice and a dash of bitters to each. Garnish with a piece of candied watermelon rind if you wish.

BASICS

The recipes in this chapter are ones that I find myself reaching for time and again. I recommend you incorporate at least some of them into your everyday repertoire. Some you may be familiar with; others you will gladly discover for the first time. From Maple-Cured Bacon (page 230) to Porcini Worcestershire Sauce (page 242), these are the staples to stock the fridge with and always have on hand as part of your cooking arsenal.

MAPLE-CURED BACON

MAKES 2 TO 4 POUNDS ● Chances are, you probably have bacon in your fridge right now. And if you're like me, you love it. Making bacon at home is not rocket science; people make a big deal about it because it takes some time and a little planning, but it is so worth it. The first step is curing pork belly with salt, sugar, maple syrup, and pink salt, which contains sodium nitrite. The main purposes of the cure are to prevent any bacterial growth on the meat and draw out some water. To store, tightly wrap in plastic and keep in the fridge for up to two weeks. If for some crazy reason you don't eat it all in a week, you can cut it into pieces, label and date it, and freeze for up to three months. Bacon is best smoked, but if you don't have a smoker at home, you can roast the pork belly in the oven as directed in the recipe. When bacon is called for in recipes throughout this book, it is uncooked.

¼ **cup kosher salt**

⅓ **cup sugar**

1¼ **tablespoons pink salt (see Note)**

¼ **cup maple syrup**

3 to 5 **pounds pork belly (see Note), skin removed**

INGREDIENT NOTES

pink salt

Pink curing salt, also referred to as saltpeter or sel rose, is popular for all types of sausage and bacon curing. The cotton candy–colored salt contains a small amount of sodium nitrite that reacts with the meat to form a more stable protein complex, making it especially resistant to oxidizing, and helps the meat to maintain a pink tinge. It is available in gourmet markets or on the Internet.

pork belly

Pork belly, which comes from the underside of the hog, is basically uncured fresh bacon. The rosy meat is marbled with fat and when baked for hours (as it is here), it becomes so custardy soft that you can literally cut it with a spoon. I have to say, the succulent and crackling fat is what makes it taste so damn delicious! A good butcher should be able to help you out when buying pork belly, and it's typically an inexpensive cut. Ask for unsalted, uncured belly, which is not the same as slab bacon or salt pork. You can often find pork belly in Asian markets.

In a glass or other nonreactive mixing bowl, combine the salt, sugar, pink salt, and maple syrup. Put the pork belly in a large resealable plastic bag. Pour in the cure, squeeze out any air in the bag, and seal; smush it around to coat the belly completely. Put the bag in a rimmed container just in case it leaks. Refrigerate for 8 days, turning the bag over every other day.

After 8 days, remove the pork belly from the cure, rinse thoroughly with cool water, and pat dry with paper towels.

Put a wire cooling rack over a baking sheet and lay the pork belly on top. If you are going to smoke the belly, allow it to dry out in the refrigerator for at least 6 hours or up to 24 hours. This is important; the meat will not take smoke until the surface is dry. Then fire up your smoker to 200°F and smoke the belly for 3 hours using your favorite wood. The internal temperature of the meat should reach 150°F. Alternatively, to roast the belly, preheat the oven to 200°F. Place the belly on a rack set in a roasting pan, and roast until the internal temperature of the meat reaches 150°F, about 3 hours.

Allow the bacon to cool to room temperature. Then wrap well with plastic wrap and store in the refrigerator for up to 2 weeks or in the freezer for up to 3 months.

PIZZA DOUGH

MAKES ABOUT 1½ POUNDS DOUGH, ENOUGH FOR FOUR 10-INCH PIZZAS

● First off, don't be scared by the idea of making pizza dough at home; it couldn't be easier. The little bit of whole wheat flour adds an earthiness to the dough, and a touch of honey adds a background sweetness that rounds out the flavors without your being able to really put your finger on it. This dough recipe is really versatile and not just for pizza. Use it to make flatbread for sandwiches and wraps, or Garlic Herb Bread Twists (page 35.)

One ¼-ounce package active dry yeast

1 teaspoon honey

2½ cups all-purpose flour, plus more for kneading

½ cup whole wheat flour

1 teaspoon kosher salt

1 tablespoon extra-virgin olive oil, plus more for the bowl

Combine the yeast, honey, and ¼ cup warm water in a small bowl; stir gently to dissolve. Let the mixture stand until the yeast starts to foam, 5 to 10 minutes.

In a mixer fitted with a dough hook, combine the flours and the salt. With the mixer running on slow speed, add the oil, yeast mixture, and ¾ cup warm water and mix until the dough comes cleanly away from the sides of the bowl, 3 to 5 minutes. (Alternatively, the dough can be made in a food processor.)

Turn the dough out onto a lightly floured clean work surface and knead by hand for just 1 to 2 minutes. The dough should be a little sticky. Gather the dough into a ball, place in a lightly oiled bowl, and turn it over to coat with the oil. Cover the dough with a clean damp towel and let it rise in a warm spot until doubled in size, about 30 minutes.

Knead the dough gently on an unfloured surface and divide into 4 equal balls; they should be about 6 ounces each and the size of large tangerines. Roll each ball under the palm of your hand until the top of the dough is smooth and firm. Cover the dough with a damp towel and let it rest for 15 to 20 minutes. The balls can now be used, wrapped in plastic and refrigerated for up to 2 days, or wrapped and frozen for up to 2 weeks.

KIMCHI

MAKES 6 CUPS ● A staple on the Korean table, kimchi is a pickled cabbage (and sometimes radish) side dish that is pungent and spicy. Traditionally, it has lots of spices and takes months to make, carefully buried in the ground to ferment. Forget all about that . . . this is a kinder, gentler version. The first thing you need to do is buy a bottle of Momoya Kimchi Base, a sweet and slightly spicy red sauce that has everything in it already. Look for it at your local Asian grocer or online. Once you have it in the fridge, you're set for a while—a little goes a long way. This recipe couldn't be easier to make but the kimchi needs at least a couple of hours to do its work, so plan ahead. I use the kimchi in practically everything from a topping on burgers to a filling for quesadillas (page 23). Spoon the kimchi into butter lettuce leaves and sprinkle with chopped peanuts for an incredibly tasty and healthy snack.

1 head Napa cabbage, halved lengthwise and cut into ½-inch pieces (3 quarts)

1 small red bell pepper, cored, seeded, and thinly sliced

1 small red onion, thinly sliced

1 small carrot, shredded

¼ cup fresh mint leaves, coarsely chopped

¼ cup fresh basil leaves, coarsely chopped

¼ cup fresh cilantro leaves, coarsely chopped

1 teaspoon grated peeled fresh ginger

Juice of 1 lime

⅓ cup Momoya Kimchi Base

In a large nonreactive bowl, toss together the cabbage, bell pepper, onion, carrot, mint, basil, and cilantro. Add the ginger, lime juice, and kimchi base; mix really well to distribute the kimchi base so it evenly coats the vegetables. Cover and refrigerate for at least 3 hours. The kimchi will keep in the refrigerator for up to 2 weeks. Let the kimchi come to room temperature before serving.

QUICK PICKLED VEGETABLES

MAKES ABOUT 2 CUPS ● Pickled vegetables are great to have in the fridge as a go-with-everything condiment; try them on sandwiches or burgers, in place of olives at a cocktail party, or alongside Falafel with Tahini Sauce (page 29). A quick brine made of rice vinegar, sugar, and water gives your favorite crisp vegetables a sweet-and-sour flavor. They'll keep for up to three months in an airtight container in the refrigerator, and the recipe can easily be doubled if you want to prepare a bigger batch. The vegetables in the recipe below are my favorites, but feel free to mix it up by adding others such as raw baby corn, zucchini, or beets. One batch of brine will be enough for any one of the suggested vegetables, below.

2 cups unseasoned rice vinegar
½ cup sugar
2 bay leaves
1 teaspoon mustard seeds

SUGGESTED VEGETABLES
2 small red onions, sliced into ¼-inch
    rounds and separated into individual
    rings
6 radishes, sliced
4 kirby cucumbers, cut into ½-inch slices
½ head cauliflower, cut into florets
2 rhubarb stalks, sliced
2 carrots, sliced

Combine the vinegar, 1 cup water, the sugar, bay leaves, and mustard seeds in a medium nonreactive pot. Slowly bring to a simmer over medium-low heat, stirring occasionally to dissolve the sugar. Put the vegetables in a heat-proof nonreactive container, pour the hot liquid on top, and toss to coat evenly; the vegetables should be completely submerged in the liquid. Cover and cool to room temperature. Chill before serving. The pickled vegetables keep for months stored covered in the refrigerator. Be sure to keep them completely submerged in the liquid.

FRESH HOMEMADE RICOTTA

MAKES ABOUT 1 QUART ● Making cheese at home is super easy. I usually salt it if I am going to use it in savory foods, such as spreads, pasta stuffings, and casseroles. For sweet dishes I might salt it just a touch, and then taste as I go. You can drizzle ricotta with honey and pair with grilled peaches or spread it on Crostini with Apricot-Thyme Jam (page 24).

1 gallon whole milk, preferably organic

1 quart buttermilk

1 tablespoon kosher salt, or more to taste

Finely grated zest of 1 lemon

½ cup heavy cream

making homemade ricotta

Always make sure your pots and utensils are super clean. Any pot or utensil with remnants of strong food flavor on it will impart that taste to the cheese. This is why you should *not* use a wooden spoon unless it is brand-new. I recommend stainless steel pans and utensils.

If you are new to making ricotta at home, use a thermometer to check how hot the milk mixture is; guessing is not a good option. Aim for 170°F to 180°F. Slow heating is the best for making curds. Don't try to rush the process or you'll end up with much less ricotta.

In a heavy-bottomed nonreactive pot, combine the whole milk, buttermilk, and salt over medium-low heat. After about 20 minutes, you will start to see steam rise from the milk; at that point give it a gentle stir with a metal spoon. After about 10 more minutes you'll begin to see curds rise to the surface (the curds are the clumpy white mass). Once you see curds floating, cook for 5 more minutes. At that point the curds will begin to sink, and that means it is time to strain the mixture.

Line a colander with a large piece of cheesecloth that has been folded over a couple of times. Set the colander in the sink. Pour the curds into the cheesecloth, leaving as much of the whey—the liquid—in the pot as possible. Gather the edges of the cloth, tie or fasten into a knot, and tie the bundle to the faucet; let the curds drip for 5 minutes.

Transfer the ricotta to a food processor and add the zest, cream, and more salt if desired. Pulse until smooth and combined. If you aren't going to use it immediately, store in an airtight container in the refrigerator. Try to eat it within 2 days; it really is best the first day you make it.

RICOTTA SALATA

For a firm ricotta that you can crumble, allow the curds to drip for at least 30 minutes. There is no need to add the zest or cream. Simply transfer to an airtight container and refrigerate.

ROASTED GARLIC

MAKES ½ CUP ROASTED WHOLE CLOVES OR ½ CUP PUREE ● Tender-sweet roasted garlic has a multitude of uses, either left whole, as in Thyme-Smoked Four-Inch Porterhouse Steak (page 168), or pureed, as in Roasted Garlic Mashed Potatoes (page 193). Keep the garlic oil for sautéing potatoes, making vinaigrettes, or brushing on fish before grilling.

1 cup peeled garlic cloves (about 40)   **About 2 cups canola oil**

Preheat the oven to 325°F.

Put the garlic cloves in a single layer in a small baking pan. Pour in enough oil to cover the garlic completely. Cover the pan tightly with aluminum foil and bake for 1 hour or until the cloves are very soft. Be sure that the garlic does not brown or, worse, burn. Cool the roasted garlic in the oil.

To make garlic puree: Remove the garlic cloves from the oil and smash the soft garlic cloves in a bowl with the back of a spoon or in a mini chopper. Add 1 to 2 tablespoons of the garlic oil and mix to combine.

The roasted garlic, whole or pureed, will keep covered in the refrigerator for up to 1 week. Store the whole cloves in the oil.

PARSLEY SAUCE

MAKES ABOUT ¾ CUP ● Like pesto, this no-cook green sauce can be used in many ways. It's awesome spooned over grilled vegetables, fish, chicken, pork, and lamb or served as a dip for crudités or focaccia. The parsley sauce can be made ahead of time and refrigerated, but is best when blended at the last minute to keep the deep green color. It's featured throughout the book in recipes from parsley croutons (page 175) and Roasted Cauliflower (page 186) to Creamy Parsley Dressing (page 87).

1 cup firmly packed fresh flat-leaf parsley
   leaves
3 tablespoons capers, drained and rinsed
2 anchovies in oil, drained

3 garlic cloves, coarsely chopped
½ teaspoon freshly ground black pepper
½ cup extra-virgin olive oil

Put the parsley, capers, anchovies, garlic, pepper, and oil in a blender. Puree until the mixture is completely smooth and bright green. The sauce should be wet and slightly soupy in consistency.

PROVENÇAL VINAIGRETTE

MAKES 2 CUPS ● This chunky, vibrantly colored vinaigrette is absolutely addictive! Each ingredient is bold on its own and together they form a tasty, slightly salty, slightly sweet, slightly acidic, rich flavor. It's outstanding on all types of fish, particularly Grilled Tuna Steak with Spring Onions (page 131).

1 beefsteak tomato, seeded and finely diced

12 pitted green olives, such as Manzanilla, finely diced

1 jarred roasted red pepper, rinsed and chopped

2 shallots, minced

¼ cup capers, drained and rinsed

½ teaspoon chopped fresh thyme

Finely grated zest and juice of ½ lemon

1½ teaspoons sherry vinegar

½ cup extra-virgin olive oil

½ teaspoon kosher salt

¼ teaspoon freshly ground black pepper

In a bowl, combine the tomato, olives, red pepper, shallots, capers, thyme, lemon zest and juice, vinegar, and oil. Stir the ingredients gently but thoroughly. Season with the salt and pepper. The vinaigrette can be made 1 day ahead of serving and will keep for 7 days covered in the fridge (if you don't eat it all by then).

PORCINI WORCESTERSHIRE SAUCE

MAKES 3 CUPS ● I think Worcestershire has incredible potential. The regular store-bought sauce has great flavor but is too thin and a little light on the palate. So what I've done is fortify the bottled stuff with more of the ingredients typically found in Worcestershire sauce to create a thicker, richer version.

1 tablespoon canola oil

½ small onion, coarsely chopped

2 garlic cloves, coarsely chopped

1 ounce dried porcini mushrooms, wiped of grit

½ navel orange, coarsely chopped (skin, pith, fruit, and all)

2 tablespoons tamarind paste or pulp

One 10-ounce bottle Worcestershire sauce

1 teaspoon kosher salt

½ teaspoon freshly ground black pepper

Put a medium nonreactive pot over medium heat and add the oil. When the oil is hot, add the onion and garlic; cook, stirring, for a couple of minutes to soften. Add the porcini and orange. Cook and stir until the porcini begin to soften, about 4 minutes. Stir in the tamarind, Worcestershire, ¾ cup water, the salt, and pepper. Reduce the heat to low, cover, and simmer for 20 minutes, until everything is soft. Puree with an immersion blender or carefully transfer to a standard blender. Serve at room temperature. Store covered in the fridge for up to 6 months.

TOMATO HARISSA

MAKES ABOUT 1½ CUPS ● Harissa is a fiery Moroccan condiment that is typically made with a variety of chiles packed with deep flavor. Incorporating tomato into store-bought harissa mellows out the heat, making this sauce even richer and more versatile. Keep it in your arsenal to boost the flavor of scrambled eggs or roasted potatoes, or stir it into your favorite vinaigrette—and it's absolutely amazing on pizza.

3 beefsteak tomatoes (about 2 pounds)	2 tablespoons harissa paste
¼ cup extra-virgin olive oil	1 teaspoon kosher salt
5 garlic cloves	½ teaspoon freshly ground black pepper
6 large basil leaves	

Bring a pot of water to a boil and prepare an ice bath. Cut a little cross mark on the bottom of the tomatoes. Immerse the tomatoes in the boiling water until the skin starts to peel away, 15 to 30 seconds. Using a slotted spoon, remove the tomatoes from the pot and transfer to the ice bath to cool quickly and stop the cooking process. Peel the tomatoes either with your hands or with a paring knife. Halve the tomatoes crosswise and squeeze out the seeds.

Place a nonreactive pot over medium heat and coat with the oil. When the oil is shimmering, add the garlic. Cook and stir until the garlic is fragrant and begins to get a little color, 1 to 2 minutes. Add the tomatoes, basil, harissa, salt, and pepper. Turn the heat up to high until the tomatoes start to release their liquid, a minute or two; then reduce the heat to medium. Cook, stirring occasionally to prevent burning, until the tomatoes start to break down and thicken, about 20 minutes.

Mash any remaining big pieces of tomato and garlic with a dough scraper or a potato masher. The sauce should remain somewhat chunky. Store covered in the fridge for a couple of days.

HABAÑERO HOT SAUCE

MAKES 3 CUPS ● For all you chile heads looking for a knockout, eye-watering, tongue-tingling sauce, here it is; you may never buy commercially made hot sauce again. But a word to the wise: proceed with caution—this is not meant for wusses. Made from habañeros, one of the fieriest chiles around, this serious sauce achieves the perfect balance between flavor and heat. It's best to protect your hands with a pair of latex gloves to keep the oils off your skin. Carrot is the secret weapon here; it not only adds amazing orange color but also gives the sauce another layer of flavor, with subtle sweetness and body. Use this hot sauce in Fried "Buffalo Style" Rabbit (page 152) or to fire up Bloody Marys or mayo. This sauce will keep practically forever!

1 tablespoon canola oil

½ white onion, coarsely chopped

6 garlic cloves, coarsely chopped

1 large carrot, chopped

1 red bell pepper, stemmed, cored, seeded, and chopped

3 habañero chiles, stemmed and coarsely chopped

1 tablespoon tomato paste

1 cup champagne vinegar

2 tablespoons agave nectar

1 tablespoon sweet smoked paprika

1 tablespoon ground cumin

1 tablespoon ground coriander

2 tablespoons kosher salt

1 tablespoon freshly ground black pepper

Put a large nonreactive pot over medium heat and coat with the oil. When the oil is hot, add the onion and garlic. Cook, stirring often, until the onion is translucent but not brown, 4 to 5 minutes. Add the carrot, bell pepper, chiles, and tomato paste and stir to combine. Pour in the vinegar and 4 cups water. Give everything a good stir and bring up to a simmer.

Add the agave, paprika, cumin, coriander, salt, and pepper. Reduce the heat to medium-low and continue to cook until all of the vegetables are super soft, about 30 minutes. Remove from the heat and let cool.

Transfer the cooled sauce to a standard blender (or use an immersion blender) and puree until smooth. Store covered in the fridge for up to 6 months.

KILLER BARBECUE SAUCE

MAKES 1 QUART ● This is my go-to sauce for ribs (see page 146) but it's also great with wings.

2 tablespoons canola oil

1 medium onion, halved and thinly sliced

4 garlic cloves, minced

1 cup hoisin sauce

½ cup apple cider vinegar

¼ cup Worcestershire sauce

3 tablespoons tomato paste

2 jarred roasted red bell peppers, rinsed and coarsely chopped

¼ cup molasses

¼ cup packed dark brown sugar

1 tablespoon chili powder

1 tablespoon sweet smoked paprika

1 tablespoon ground cumin

1 teaspoon kosher salt

½ teaspoon freshly ground black pepper

Put a medium pot over medium heat and coat with the oil. When the oil is hot, add the onion and garlic. Cook and stir for a minute until soft. Add the hoisin, vinegar, Worcestershire, tomato paste, roasted peppers, molasses, sugar, chili powder, paprika, cumin, salt, pepper, and 1 cup water. Reduce the heat to low and simmer, stirring occasionally, until the sauce is thick, 20 minutes. Puree with an immersion blender or transfer to a standard blender. Let cool completely. The sauce will keep covered in the refrigerator for up to 6 months.

BEST MAYONNAISE

MAKES 3 CUPS ● Because I use whole soft-boiled eggs and not just the yolks, this simple recipe makes the thickest, best mayo that you can imagine. It keeps for up to a week in the fridge.

2 teaspoons kosher salt

3 large eggs

1½ tablespoons Dijon mustard

2 cups canola oil

Fill a pot with enough water to cover the eggs plus 1 inch. Add 1 teaspoon of salt. (This will make peeling the eggs easier once they're cooked.) Bring the water to a boil.

Carefully lower the eggs into the boiling water. Simmer the eggs for 4 minutes, until soft boiled. Lift the eggs out of the water with a slotted spoon and immediately run under cold water. (This will stop the eggs from cooking in their own heat and will prevent a discoloration of the egg yolk that sometimes forms.)

Crack the eggs on the counter and scoop them out into a food processor. Add the mustard and the remaining 1 teaspoon salt. Puree the eggs and, while the motor is running, slowly drizzle in the oil through the feed tube. The mayo will be super thick.

ACKNOWLEDGMENTS

IT'S ALMOST UNBELIEVABLE TO ME when I think of what went into making this cookbook. After all, it's just food! I am surrounded by such incredibly talented people, and so I am genuinely happy—and proud—to recognize them here.

My wife, Tamara, for standing by me through the best and worst of times. And loving me all the while. I love you too!

Ella, for reminding me to be better, so I don't embarrass her.

Lulu, for her sweet insight, and for questioning everything!

Harry, for goofing around, and reminding us all that it's OK.

My mom, Judy, for letting me cut the white bread into cubes for Thanksgiving.

My dad, Marvin, for his simple perspective.

Sunil Bhatt, the best cook I know, for his full-on support. Always!

Frank Crispo, for teaching me how to work fast. Let's go!

Aliza Green, for giving me my first kitchen job.

Wolfgang Puck, for opening my eyes to the world of flavor.

Maida Heatter, for all the skinny peanut wafers over the years, and for teaching me the importance of a good recipe.

Hedy Goldsmith, for inspiring me to be better (than her)!

Jackie Sayet, for an endless stream of great ideas and for keeping me organized.

Bradley, Thomas, and Prudent and the entire kitchen staff at Michael's Genuine Food & Drink, for making me look good!

Charles Bell and the entire front-of-house staff at Michael's Genuine Food & Drink, for their tireless level of service and for making the entire kitchen staff (including me!) look good.

Gabriele Marewski, for growing beautiful things, and for giving me tea when I don't feel great.

Jorge Figueroa, for the best local fish.

Tina and Michael Borek, Margie Pikarsky, Hani Kouri, Jodi Swank, Trish Strawn, Green Dean, and all the local South Florida growers and producers, for their hard work and commitment to great food.

Larry Carrino, Karen Barofsky, and Susan Brustman from Brustman Carrino Public Relations for introducing me to JoAnn Cianciulli, and the rest of the world!

JoAnn Cianciulli, for capturing my voice.

Ben Fink, for being so patient and an incredibly talented photographer.

Rudolf Kohn, the best prop stylist I know!

Betty Rosado, for the use of her amazing studio and for her incredible input.

Gary Rosenburg, for the most beautiful pottery.

Doris Cooper, for giving me this opportunity, and Rica Allannic, for making it happen.

My investors, for taking a shot in the dark, literally.

My regular and irregular customers, for making themselves at home in our dining room as if it were their own.

—MICHAEL SCHWARTZ

LOVING WHAT I DO EVERY DAY is the absolute greatest joy in my life. Writing cookbooks and producing food television shows is a hybrid career I created for myself that characterizes my passion for cooking in a unique way. As a result, I'm fortunate to collaborate closely with the top talent in the culinary world. One of the things I've learned from working with chefs is that there are many different ways to cook great food. I truly feel like an interpreter, taking the language of food together with the chef's philosophy behind it and joining them on the page.

This book would not have been possible without the intelligence and loyalty of my coauthor, superstar chef Michael Schwartz. Michael, thank you for letting me climb inside your brilliant brain and put your full and delicious thoughts on paper. You are a great professional mentor and it's been a true joy to work with you on countless levels.

I must give a shout-out to the talented people who contributed to this book in one way or another:

Larry Carrino, Karen Barofsky, and Susan Brustman, for making it happen and having the keen ability to recognize the right fit between chef and writer.

GM Charles Bell, for that wicked laugh and for welcoming me into the family with open arms.

Pastry chef Hedy Goldsmith, for being the real deal—you're an esteemed woman in a league all your own.

Ryan Goodspeed, for fortifying the subtleties of mixology and treating the art of drink as seriously as food.

Jaime and the whole MGFD team, for adopting me as part of the crew. You are best at what you do and are simply incredible to watch in action.

Ben Fink, for being a true master at the craft of food photography; you are as much fun as you are accomplished.

Rudolf Kohn, for excellent taste, candid honesty, and for weaving the food and mood together effortlessly with every tabletop.

David Domedion, for testing the recipes down to the last grain of salt and for possessing such an impeccable palate.

Ingrid Hoffmann, for welcoming me into her comfortable casa and creating a Miami chica retreat.

Rica Allannic, our skillful editor, for pushing my writing (and me) to a higher level.

Angela Miller, my top-notch literary agent, for always telling it like it is.

My mother, Gloria, for embracing my quirky career and for letting me do the cooking.

My aunt Grace, for positively shaping the woman I am today, and the child I was then.

Pat Sanders, for entering my life unexpectedly and enriching it beyond measure.

Monique and Shari, my lifelong girlfriends, for helping me keep it all together.

—JOANN CIANCIULLI

INDEX